Why Bad Looks Good is a powerful, highly practical primer on life's most important lessons. In a world where dangers abound, Dr. Patrick's biblically grounded wisdom provides indispensable guidance for navigating the perilous tempests of daily life. She helps readers master the art of discernment and learn to detect red flags, spot green lights, and seize golden opportunities.

Judge Ken Starr

For years I have said that the number one thing I pray for is discernment. If I have discernment, then so many other things fall into place. Just like Solomon, who prayed for wisdom, which brought him other blessings, discernment is what we all need most today in this era of misinformation and intentional disinformation. Wendy Patrick—with not only a law degree but also seminary and doctorate degrees—is academically well qualified. Her spiritual discernment, emotional maturity, and street savviness qualify her to write this book even more. When Wendy speaks, we all need to listen. When Wendy writes, we all need to read. Read anything she writes. Especially this.

Dr. Jim Garlow
CEO of Well Versed

I can't think of a timelier book on the issue of deception in a world that's fed a steady diet of it. Dr. Patrick's career as a prosecuting attorney brings the harsh truths of her experiences as vivid examples of how prevalent a problem it is. The sound wisdom within these pages is not only timely but could also literally spare you from lifelong grief and regret. A must-read!

Dr. Frank Correa
Academic Dean and Professor of Theology and Apologetics, Veritas International University

I can't think of anyone better qualified to write this book than Wendy Patrick, whose years as a defense attorney, district attorney, and criminal justice consultant make her an expert at identifying the bad disguised as the good. Her readable style, interesting case studies, and deep draw from the biblical wisdom tradition make this a fascinating read and a helpful guide.

Mark L. Strauss, PhD
Author of *Four Portraits, One Jesus* and *How to Read the Bible in Changing Times*
Professor of New Testament, Bethel Seminary

Today it's more important than ever to be discerning, clear-headed, and just plain wise. But it's difficult to do this since so much deception and wishful thinking are out there. As someone who has taught Christians how to think clearly, I believe *Why Bad Looks Good* can help us make good biblical decisions.

Gary Zacharias
Apologetics Ministry Leader

Wendy Patrick brings a unique focus to living wisely as a Christian. Her experience as an attorney, her exposition of Scripture influenced by her theological training, and her interaction with thousands of people through her public speaking all come together in this book to provide a great deal of wisdom on the complex issue of applying biblical guidance to the challenges that Christians face in life. It's a distinct contribution to Christian literature.

Myron S. Steeves
Dean Emeritus, Trinity Law School

WHY BAD LOOKS GOOD

Biblical Wisdom to Make Smart
Choices in Life, Love, and Friendship

WENDY PATRICK

BroadStreet
PUBLISHING

BroadStreet Publishing® Group, LLC
Savage, Minnesota, USA
BroadStreetPublishing.com

Why Bad Looks Good: Biblical Wisdom to Make Smart Choices in Life, Love, and Friendship
Copyright © 2023 Wendy Patrick

9781424564774 (hardcover)
9781424564781 (ebook)

Stock or custom editions of BroadStreet Publishing titles may be purchased in bulk for educational, business, ministry, fundraising, or sales promotional use. For information, please email orders@broadstreetpublishing.com.

Cover and interior by Garborg Design Works | garborgdesign.com

Printed in China

23 24 25 26 27 5 4 3 2 1

To my mother, Elizabeth Patrick, and my sister,
Jennifer Patrick. The loving, godly role models
who inspire my Christian walk every day
as we navigate the adventures of life together.

CONTENTS

Foreword 9

Introduction 12

Chapter 1   The Deception of Public Perception 18

Chapter 2   When Bad Appears Beautiful 24

Chapter 3   The Deception of Dress 29

Chapter 4   When Bad Sounds Good 35

Chapter 5   When You Hear What You Want to Hear 40

Chapter 6   The Halo of Hypocrisy 47

Chapter 7   The Fallacy of Feelings 54

Chapter 8   When Bad Feels Good 62

Chapter 9   When Haste Makes Waste 68

Chapter 10   The Allure of Idolatry 73

Chapter 11   When Less Looks like More 80

Chapter 12   When Risky Looks Rewarding 86

Chapter 13   When Darkness Looks Desirable 93

Chapter 14   When Lust Feels like Love 98

Chapter 15   When Immoral Seems Normal 105

Chapter 16   When Frenemies Look like Friends............. 111

Chapter 17   The Optics of Occupation 118

Chapter 18   When Credentials Do Not Reveal Character 125

Chapter 19   The Ruse of Reputation 130

Chapter 20   The Illusion of Intelligence 136

Chapter 21   The Fantasy of First Impressions 140

Chapter 22   The Perils of Power 145

Chapter 23   The Rapture of Riches 150

Chapter 24   The Lure of Luxury 157

Chapter 25   When Busyness Looks like Business 162

Chapter 26   The Temptations of Technology 167

Conclusion   173

Acknowledgments 181

Endnotes   183

About the Author 190

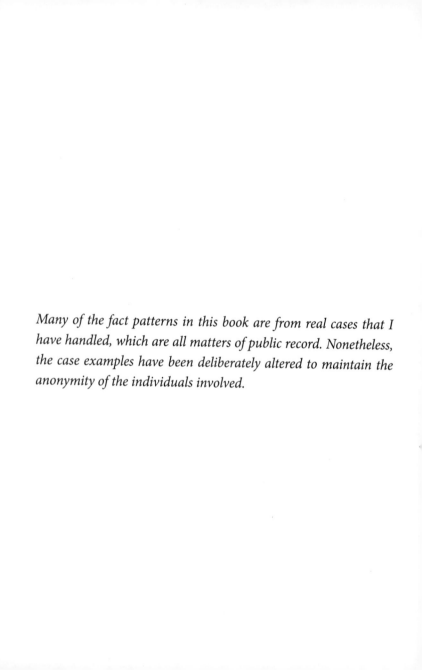

Many of the fact patterns in this book are from real cases that I have handled, which are all matters of public record. Nonetheless, the case examples have been deliberately altered to maintain the anonymity of the individuals involved.

FOREWORD

In so many conversations, nationally and internationally, I have heard people express concern about the "topsy turvy" world in which we live. One often hears something like this: "It seems like people do not have any common sense anymore." Did we ever? Nevertheless, the upside-down state of things may truly be worse now.

Wendy Patrick has seen the liar, the thief, the charlatan, the actor, the deceiver, the innocent, the broken, the abused, and the devious. She has faced criminality, domestic violence, and first-degree murder cases, and at times she has witnessed tragic injustice. The innocent do not always go free, and the guilty are not always sentenced—both of which illustrate how the world is indeed upside down. Mixed with this darkness and maelstrom, however, are the selfless, amazing individuals who have startled Wendy by their ability to brighten any environment, shining like the aurora in the midnight sky. Their caring hearts bless this planet and make our world truly lovable. All that is to say that

Wendy's experience has shown her virtually every side of the spectrum of "good" and "bad."

I have known Wendy for approximately two decades and have seen her incredible expertise in action and her dedication as a lawyer, prosecutor, and defense attorney. I also know her accolades, such as being named "Public Lawyer of the Year" by the California State Bar Public Law Section. She even pivoted beyond law and attended theological seminary, graduating summa cum laude, and earned a master of divinity in San Diego and then a doctorate in theology from the University of Wales Trinity Saint David.

Many people tend to see the world and others through only single or dual prisms, but Wendy has a multifaceted perspective, which she reflects and shares in this work, *Why Bad Looks Good*. Whereas few people can straddle the bridge between the legal world, the spiritual world, and all the other pieces that make up real life, Wendy does so with aplomb. She anchors her life and writing in quality relationships with examples of positive care for others and creation and guides readers by the truth of Scripture, reflected through life stories and principles.

As the subtitle of this book promises, Wendy shares the simple, practical truths of the Bible and clearly delineates specific approaches for positive everyday living. And the illustrations she shares of real people and real experiences are not only amazingly appropriate and adroitly placed, but they also teach principles that any man or woman can utilize. She further lays out those steps of life that present opportunities for success individually, in relationships, and in business. In doing so, Wendy paints a picture of a balanced life, the daily walk that brings joy from beginning to end, and opportunities by faith for cloverleaf movements on the highway of life, helping readers get back on track and move past any momentary failure.

In reading this flowing blend of storytelling, law, and theological truths as only Wendy can depict, the haze of this world clears away. One begins to see the light burn off the mist and finds clarity in perception, taking in a true view of a fulfilling existence.

Tom Phillips
Vice President
Billy Graham Evangelistic Association

INTRODUCTION

Woe to those who call evil good and good evil,
who put darkness for light and light for darkness,
who put bitter for sweet and sweet for bitter.
ISAIAH 5:20

Have you ever misjudged a person or a situation that appeared desirable only for it to end in disaster? Has a friend or love interest ever betrayed you? Did you take a chance on a seemingly lucrative business venture that turned out to be a bust, or did you learn the hard way that living dangerously and taking physical risks can end in injury? If you find yourself answering yes to any of these questions, you're far from alone.

As a career prosecutor, I have decades of experience working with victims and witnesses from all walks of life who became involved with manipulators and offenders who didn't seem "dangerous." On the contrary, others perceived these people as desirable. I have realized over the years how frequently people miss red flags because an attractive, alluring package of qualities or circumstances shroud those flags.

My heart for ministry and for sparing future victims from the hazards of misperception sparked my desire to help set the record straight with *Why Bad Looks Good*. *Why Bad Looks Good* is also the title of a column that I have been writing for almost a decade for the psychology and human behavior media platform *Psychology Today*. In my column (and in this book), I discuss and explain the emotional and psychological reasons behind our attraction to harmful, hazardous people, opportunities, and circumstances.

The Benefit of Biblical Wisdom

We encounter heartbreaking experiences every day. A young woman receives a phone call while shopping for her wedding dress, and the caller alleges that the woman's fiancé has been unfaithful. A veteran employee of a bank discovers majorly concerning accounting irregularities that implicate his boss, requiring him to decide if, when, and how to blow the whistle. A father learns that not only does his seven-year-old daughter have a rare form of cancer requiring immediate hospitalization, but he must also be the one to break the devastating news to her. These matters of life, death, betrayal, and adversity require us to make important decisions. Where can we turn for advice?

The self-help aisles at our local bookstores are full of worldly ideas. Ironically, what we won't find within those aisles is the most popular and successful self-help book in the world: the Bible. The Bible is free, easily accessible online, and routinely dispensed at churches and religious institutions. Its wisdom is free for the taking: "If any of you lacks wisdom, you should ask God, who gives generously to all without finding fault" (James 1:5). Some people write off the Bible as a list of "Thou Shall Nots," but nothing could be further from the truth.

Unlike the well-intended but unpersuasive "because I said so" rationale that some parents rely on, the Bible articulates both rhyme and reason for its guidelines. For example, it advises us not to associate with hot-tempered people lest we learn their ways and become like them (see Proverbs 22:24–25). Husbands and wives are discouraged from depriving their spouses of physical affection except by agreement lest they fall into temptation (see 1 Corinthians 7:4–5). Children are instructed to obey their parents, reminding them of the first commandment to do so "so that it may go well with you and that you may enjoy long life on the earth" (Ephesians 6:1–3). Pairing rules with rationales not only helps us better understand their purpose, but it also helps us identify and apply the wisdom behind the warnings.

Biblical wisdom is drastically different from worldly wisdom. As the Lord declares, "For my thoughts are not your thoughts, neither are your ways my ways…As the heavens are higher than the earth, so are my ways higher than your ways and my thoughts than your thoughts" (Isaiah 55:8–9). Unlike worldly advice, God's advice is perfect because he created you and knows everything about you. Before a word is on your tongue, he knows what it is (see Psalm 139:4). He knows what you need before you ask (see Matthew 6:8). He even knows how many hairs are on your head (see Luke 12:7). And because God created everyone, he knows just as much about everyone else as he does about you, including why some people, unfortunately, are not to be trusted.

Developing Discernment

We are drawn to talent, wealth, and beauty, yet all of those things come from God. And although incredibly appealing, desires of the flesh and eyes are worldly and unspiritual (see 1 John 2:16). Deception impacts perception, making it more difficult to identify a smooth operator's true motives. That's why it's imperative for us to be able to distinguish flash from substance whenever we find ourselves impressed by someone or something. To avoid being manipulated by ulterior motives, we have to learn how to recognize authenticity. In short, we have to learn the art of discernment: "Discretion will protect you, and understanding will guard you" (Proverbs 2:11).

Perhaps the most common obstacle to developing discernment today is distraction. Many of us float through our days distracted by our own thoughts or the text messages, alerts, and notifications competing for our attention. We lack the necessary concentration and diligence to spot anything out of the ordinary should it cross our path, and the cumulative effect of distraction causes us to miss red flags, green lights, and golden opportunities.

First and foremost, discernment requires preparation. When we first turn to God for guidance, we receive unique instruction: "Call to me and I will answer you and tell you great and unsearchable things you do not know" (Jeremiah 33:3). Once we submit to God's guidance, we are prepared and protected by the armor of God, which allows us to practice discernment whenever we encounter new people and circumstances. And by practicing biblical discernment, we learn in time to distinguish the good from the bad, which facilitates health, hope, and happiness in every area of our lives.

Learning to discern when bad looks good also requires patience and perseverance. We may not always get it right, but we gain confidence and strength each and every time we slow down and focus on making a conscious, wise decision. This confidence and strength also protect us from getting "tossed back and forth by the waves, and blown here and there" by every type of teaching or the "cunning and craftiness of people" who deceive us through scheming (Ephesians 4:14).

In *Why Bad Looks Good*, we'll explore Scripture and biblical wisdom that will enhance your perception of people and circumstances. We'll also use practical, relatable, real-life examples to illustrate how you can apply divine wisdom in every area of your life in order to make wise choices. From money to marriage, health to happiness, and gossip to greed, learn to live peacefully but proactively, compassionately yet carefully. Transform your rose-colored glasses to reading glasses and develop a fresh, uplifting perspective of the people and world around you.

CHAPTER 1

THE DECEPTION OF PUBLIC PERCEPTION

The god of this age has blinded the minds of unbelievers,
so that they cannot see the light of the gospel
that displays the glory of Christ.

2 CORINTHIANS 4:4

We live in a world where bad not only looks good but is also actually described as good. Where naughty is marketed as nice by advertisers intentionally showcasing the provocative nature of the products they sell. Using words and images that present products as "dangerous," "forbidden," "wicked," and "guilty," they intentionally cater to the dark side of humanity. Most people have become desensitized to such labeling and promotion. But to what end?

Consider the people you follow on social media and why. Do you find them inspirational or interesting? Are you motivated by moral conviction or morbid curiosity? Your answers predict the influence such content has on your life.

Following internet influencers or Hollywood heroes might mean you also emulate the lifestyle they lead—for better or for worse. We live in an era where we are consistently exposed to alternative lifestyles and bombarded with advertisements and sexualized portrayals of modern behavior. In reality, however, many trending social "norms" are anything but.

When Abnormal Seems Normal

Society often values things that the Bible does not. For example, most every culture emphasizes appearance. This focus on the physical is celebrated in countless ways, such as beauty contests like Miss America and Miss Universe, where the most attractive woman in a region is selected from each city, state, and country in the world. Social media influencers seduce the impressionable by glamourizing their lifestyles and using unrealistic filters to enhance their appearance, making their choices seem acceptable, if not aspirational. Popular television shows focus on handsome men as well, often within the context of having a harem of women competing for one man's attention. Once a couple ties the knot, we move on to programs featuring "real" housewives and exploiting the manufactured dramas of ultrarich fractured families—not quite the fairy-tale romance and happily-ever-after storylines our precious young people were exposed to in years past.

Sure, provocative shows focus on ratings, not role modeling, but Hollywood portrayals inarguably influence perception and popularity. And unlike in a court of law, where a judge controls the presented evidence, in the court of public opinion, people choose the content they want to consume and the voices they want to listen to. They mindlessly follow whatever happens to be trending without understanding that repeating an idea might make it popular.

Normalizing and legitimizing maladaptive, harmful thoughts and behaviors create a dangerous environment of permissive immorality. Whether in terms of infidelity, dishonesty, or depravity, marketing malevolence is no less harmful to public morality simply because it is portrayed as normal.

Some people don't even try to hide their prideful nonconformity. Peter warns us about bold and brazen personalities who openly practice deceit and debauchery. "Their idea of pleasure is to carouse in broad daylight. They are blots and blemishes, reveling in their pleasures while they feast with you. With eyes full of adultery, they never stop sinning; they seduce the unstable; they are experts in greed" (2 Peter 2:13–14).

Even when abominable behavior damages life and health, such as when God withheld the lifegiving showers from Israel, the behavior continues unabated: "Yet you have the brazen look of a prostitute; you refuse to blush with shame" (Jeremiah 3:3).

We see similar behavior today— people living in depravity, behaving in deceitful, wicked, greedy, arrogant, and boastful fashions, knowing their behavior is sinful but continuing in it and encouraging others who behave the same way (see Romans 1:29–32). We are wise to carefully consider whom we follow and where they may be leading us.

Following the Crowd…Right off a Cliff

When I was growing up, our elders warned us of participating in activities and behaviors merely because everyone else was doing it. They'd ask us the classic question, "If everyone jumped off a cliff, would you do it too?" Things are no different today in terms of trends; except in our world of social media, ideas spread easier and so much faster. The internet truly is filled with videos that make extreme behavior look mainstream. People are then quick to jump off the proverbial trendy cliff by jumping to the wrong conclusions. They fall victim to false information because it's paired with a hashtag and shared by "friends," "fans," and "followers" who have no more wisdom than they do.

Social media also promotes a misplaced sense of safety in numbers. Wayward souls seeking wild or dangerous experiences can assure themselves that "everyone's doing it" or "I'm not the only one." And unfortunately, whether someone is seeking to learn how to bake a cake or build a bomb, a supportive virtual community is ready to assist. Before their killing sprees, many school shooters and mass murderers connected with like-minded criminals online, some of whom encouraged their horrific massacres.

> Social media promotes a misplaced sense
> of safety in numbers.

When deciding whether to follow social media influencers, consider what their posts reveal. Influencers leading alternative lifestyles can lead us right off the beaten path and into dangerous territory both physically and spiritually. Despite the promise of a bright and shiny future, one in which your life mirrors theirs, beware of the light at the end of the tunnel that might just turn out to be an oncoming train.

The Bible, by contrast, will keep you on the right track, as God's Word is "a lamp for my feet, a light on my path" (Psalm 119:105). The things that come from the Spirit of God can only be discerned through the Spirit, not through the world. As 1 Corinthians 2:14 reads, "The person without the Spirit does not accept the things that come from the Spirit of God but considers them foolishness, and cannot understand them because they are discerned only through the Spirit."

Truth Is Always #Trending

In my profession, the laws change every year. This requires us to keep up to date with the latest legislation and propositions in order to stay on top of the ever-evolving legal landscape. Social movements and ideas endorsed by airbrushed influencers are also constantly in flux, depending on whatever tweets, shares, and social media posts are currently trending. In stark contrast, the Bible does not change. Biblical truth is timeless: "Jesus Christ is the same yesterday and today and forever" (Hebrews 13:8). He is "the way and the truth and the life" (John 14:6).

Those who look the other way or go with the crowd despite knowing better are reminded that evil spreads when good people do nothing and remain bystanders. The book of James advises us that it is sinful to know the good we ought to do but not do it (see James 4:17). Sharing biblical wisdom is distributing timeless truths designed not to highlight the latest fads but to remind ourselves, loved ones, and others of eternal facts. Sharing truth in this fashion is like tossing a life preserver to people who are confused, lost, depressed, or otherwise "tossed back and forth by the waves, and blown here and there by every wind of teaching" (Ephesians 4:14). Sharing the gospel provides people peace, comfort, and solid ground to stand on in the midst of storms.

CHAPTER 2

WHEN BAD
APPEARS BEAUTIFUL

Stop judging by mere appearances,
but instead judge correctly.
JOHN 7:24

Have you ever seen someone from across the room and done a double take? Not because you thought you knew them, but because you wanted to. Not because you assumed they were good, but because they were good looking. Looking is the first step. Next you ask someone, "Who is that?" Or you cross the room to find out. Attraction prompts interaction. But observer beware: what you see is not always what you get.

Many of the sexual predators I have prosecuted over the years were worthy of a double take, as evidenced by the reaction I observed from many of my jurors when the defendant was introduced. Lady Justice is blind; jurors are not. Despite eleven out of twelve jurors who were ready to convict, one woman hung a jury in a sexual assault case and chose to protect an attractive defendant she bonded with during the trial. The defendant had initiated flirtatious eye contact with her, and afterward, the woman asked me how to contact the man in jail.

Judging by appearances is not a new phenomenon. When Samuel visited Jesse of Bethlehem, because the Lord had chosen one of Jesse's sons to be the next king, he viewed the first son and thought he was the one, perhaps believing he "looks like a king." However, God spoke to Samuel, saying, "Do not consider his appearance or his height, for I have rejected him," explaining that "people look at the outward appearance, but the LORD looks at the heart" (1 Samuel 16:7). Consider that the Lord's actual choice for the new king, David, the youngest of Jesse's sons, was also famously underestimated as "only a young man" when he boldly offered to fight mighty Goliath (1 Samuel 17:33). Misjudging ability based on appearances was also the downfall of the Israelites, who would have entered the promised land forty years earlier if they had not underestimated their ability to overpower the inhabitants, whom they described as powerful, strong, and of "great size" (Numbers 13:31–33).

Although the Bible clearly recognizes physical beauty, attractiveness does not always equate with righteousness: "Your heart became proud on account of your beauty, and you corrupted your wisdom because of your splendor" (Ezekiel 28:17).

Consider the physical description of Absalom, who revolted against his father King David: "In all Israel there was not a man so highly praised for his handsome appearance as Absalom. From the top of his head to the sole of his foot there was no blemish in him" (2 Samuel 14:25).

Compare that to the prophetic description of Jesus: "He had no beauty or majesty to attract us to him, nothing in his appearance that we should desire him" (Isaiah 53:2). The danger when faced with physical beauty is that when the view is good, we look but don't listen. Big mistake.

When a Halo Is a Hologram

Have you ever had a crush on an acquaintance you find attractive? Someone you knew from your workplace, neighborhood, school, or perhaps someone on the periphery of your social circle? Having a crush on someone you are attracted to but don't know well allows your mind to fill in the gaps. We are quick to crown attractive people with a halo, assuming the best of them. But should we?

The *halo effect* refers to our tendency to favorably misjudge attractive people, often attributing to them a wide variety of positive qualities they do not actually have. We assume that an attractive woman is a good mother and a loyal wife. We imagine she is compassionate, kind, tender, and generous with her time and money…without any basis in fact for our assumptions. Similarly, we assume that a handsome man is a hard worker, confident, trustworthy, and a positive role model. We figure he is probably a talented athlete as well. In short, we tend to give good-looking people the benefit of the doubt, again without any rational basis for our optimism. I had one juror admit she could not convict a baby-faced defendant because of his heavenly appearance. "He looks like an angel!" she said.

We are warned in 1 Peter 5:8 to be sober-minded and alert because our enemy, the devil, "prowls around like a roaring lion looking for someone to devour." But he doesn't look like a roaring lion because that would scare off his prey. He looks like the manipulators and sexual predators I prosecute: attractive and charismatic. "And no wonder, Paul reminds us, because Satan "masquerades as an angel of light" (2 Corinthians 11:14).

Because beauty is skin deep, attractive but bad people are often favorably misjudged. Their ability to manipulate and exploit creates the crime and calamity that keeps me employed as a prosecutor. But life would be much easier if victims could see clearly from the beginning and spare themselves both harm and heartbreak.

> Because beauty is skin deep,
> attractive but bad people are often favorably misjudged.

When Beautiful Is Good

Solomon portrays his lover in the book Song of Songs using many vivid descriptors of beauty, including "eyes like doves," a pleasant voice, and a lovely face (Song of Solomon 1:15; 2:14 NLT). Moses was described as a child as "beautiful" (Hebrews 11:23 ESV). Joseph, the most favored son of the patriarch Jacob, was "well-built and handsome" (Genesis 39:6).

The Bible describes beauty beyond physical terms too. "How beautiful on the mountains are the feet of those who bring good news, who proclaim peace, who bring good tidings, who proclaim salvation" (Isaiah 52:7). "Those who look to him are radiant; their faces are never covered with shame" (Psalm 34:5).

Thankfully, many people are indeed beautiful both inside and out. Shining with love and kindness, they are attractive visually, verbally, and behaviorally. Just take the time to verify that what you see and assume about a person is, in fact, as good as it looks.

CHAPTER 3

THE DECEPTION OF DRESS

Watch out for false prophets.
They come to you in sheep's clothing,
but inwardly they are ferocious wolves.
MATTHEW 7:15

Many jurors come to court expecting to hear a case involving shoplifting, vandalism, or driving under the influence. Consequently, as a career sex crime prosecutor, I am all too familiar with the expressions of horror that quickly spread across the faces of the men and women in the jury box when the judge reads the charges in one of my cases. Child molestation. Incest. Rape. Murder. Many jurors admit they could not listen to a case involving that kind of evidence. Some hold stereotypes about the kind of people capable of committing those types of crimes, including what they would look like.

If a defendant is charged with being a sexual predator, jurors expect to see a creepy-looking ice cream truck driver in a trench coat with pockets full of candy. Instead, they see a handsome man dressed to impress in a pin-striped business suit with a monogrammed briefcase. Some of the most dangerous people I have prosecuted were also the best dressed, looking like they should be trading on Wall Street rather than testifying on a witness stand.

Yet these wolves in sharp clothing are dressed for deception; that is precisely how they got away with committing their crimes. Sure enough, speaking with my jurors after trial, some admit that their verdicts were based not on the evidence presented but on the appearance of the defendant. "He didn't look like a criminal; he looked like a lawyer," one juror explained after an acquittal. The irony was not lost on me.

Some jurors can't tell the defendant from the defense attorney until the parties are formally introduced. The jurors just see two men in sharp suits sitting side by side. Women can dress to deceive and distract as well. I have had jurors completely ignore testimony from the witness stand while smiling at the pretty woman, clad in polka dots and pearls, sitting at the defendant's table with charges of robbing a bank, having sex with her students, or worse.

If my jurors were at the Oscars, they probably couldn't distinguish Hollywood stars from dazzling, dressed-to-the-nines offenders either. That is because fashion-based favoritism is subconscious. The book of James cautions readers not to bestow special attention by offering premium seating to a man wearing fine clothes and a gold ring over a poor man wearing old, filthy clothes (see James 2:2–4). We are reminded that the body is about more than clothes (see Matthew 6:25). When we judge character through clothing-based conclusions, we are often wrong.

When Credibility Is a Costume

One advantage of having my office in a courthouse is the security detail downstairs. No one can just stop by to see me without being verified and vetted by a trained security professional, which is a comforting perk as a prosecutor. But threat assessment is only as good as the perception of the assessor. If a dangerous person looks distinguished and conventionally respectable, then their professional packaging conceals any and all potential danger.

I have prosecuted individuals who masqueraded as everything from army veterans to veteran cops. Having watched enough military documentaries or crime dramas to know the lingo and lay of the land, they were able to talk the talk and walk the walk. Costumes are easy to find, and inexpensive business cards are almost literally a dime a dozen.

False fronts are unfortunately effective, as demonstrated during some of the live suspect lineups I have conducted. A victim who observes that "they all look alike" is often reacting to the matching outfits, and yet that is exactly how well-dressed defendants operate. A cloak of credibility provides cover to commit crime.

Dressed for the Occasion

When I was a criminal defense attorney, I wanted my clients to look their best for court. If a client was in custody, I could play more of an active role in suit selection to help them dress for success. Otherwise, I had to rely on their judgment, which was not always a safe bet. Some waltzed in looking like a character straight off the set of *The Godfather*—not a good look if they were facing gang-related allegations. Others wore their Sunday best only to have an honest, blunt juror tell the judge that "anyone who would wear that shirt to court is definitely guilty of something." Beginning a criminal trial with a fashion felony is not a good start.

Assuming a person has the liberty to choose their own clothing, we can learn much about them from their fashion choices and how they choose to dress for a certain occasion. And I don't just mean wearing white shoes after Labor Day. A wealthy A-lister who shows up at the Oscars in old jeans and a ripped jacket makes a loud statement without ever saying a word. What impressions would you have of someone who showed up to a first date with you wearing a wrinkled shirt with fresh food stains on it?

In the parable of the wedding feast, when a king hosted a banquet and invited everyone his servants could find, he noticed a man among the guests who was not wearing wedding clothes and asked him how he managed to get in (see Matthew 22:1–12). Because of the expectations and impressions that clothing signifies with respect to material and context, we should take note not only of what someone wears but also where they're wearing it and why.

> Take note not only of what someone wears but also where they're wearing it and why.

The Maiden in Modest Clothing

Unlike the wolf in sharp clothing, many good people dress stylishly but modestly. Speaking to women, the apostle Peter states: "Your beauty should not come from outward adornment, such as elaborate hairstyles and the wearing of gold jewelry or fine clothes. Rather, it should be that of your inner self, the unfading beauty of a gentle and quiet spirit, which is of great worth in God's sight" (1 Peter 3:3–4).

This does not mean that women shouldn't wear jewelry, dress fashionably, or visit the salon. Nor does it mean we should automatically be suspicious of attractive people. Most everyone wants to look their best, but further analysis must be considered. For example, does someone want to look good—or specifically better than someone else? Is a woman who shows up at a party dripping with diamonds showcasing warmth or wealth? As Proverbs 31:30 reads, "Charm is deceptive, and beauty is fleeting; but a woman who fears the Lord is to be praised."

And speaking of wealth, you can learn a lot about a person by how much they spend on clothes and jewelry or elective cosmetic procedures in the futile pursuit of eternal youth. This is one facet of practicing discernment—considering *why* people make the beauty and fashion choices they do as well as their choice in attitude and behavior. This type of discernment relays information about a person's priorities, profession, and personal beliefs. In short, outward ornamentation can be illusory, while spectacular beauty often comes in a modest package.

WHEN BAD SOUNDS GOOD

His talk is smooth as butter,
yet war is in his heart;
his words are more soothing than oil,
yet they are drawn swords.
PSALM 55:21

As a trial attorney, I speak for a living. Silver-tongued advocates are celebrated for their ability to persuade judges and juries. Some learn the art of articulation in law school; others are born with the gift of gab. Smooth talkers sound sensible and smart, but sometimes bad sounds brilliant. Some of you might attend meetings where a know-it-all board member always has her hand raised, seeking to dominate the discussion. Or you might remember a high school classmate who could talk his way out of anything, whether caught ditching school or "losing" homework.

Like every other talent, one's speaking ability can be used for good or for evil. Paul warns, "Let no one deceive you with empty words, for because of such things God's wrath comes on those who are disobedient" (Ephesians 5:6). Some people cannot be trusted: "Their throats are open graves; their tongues practice deceit. The poison of vipers is on their lips" (Romans 3:13). Or as Proverbs 26 reads, "Like a coating of silver dross on earthenware are fervent lips with an evil heart. Enemies disguise themselves with their lips, but in their hearts they harbor deceit. Though their speech is charming, do not believe them" (vv. 23–25).

We are warned to avoid being misled through polished pearls of persuasion: "See to it that no one takes you captive through hollow and deceptive philosophy, which depends on human tradition and the elemental spiritual forces of this world rather than on Christ" (Colossians 2:8). Peter warns about false prophets and teachers, covertly introducing "destructive heresies" yet gaining followers, and in their greed, exploiting others with "fabricated stories" (2 Peter 2:1–3).

In all matters, we are well advised to consider the foundation supporting any claim. And we are encouraged to listen to different viewpoints and avoid rushing to judgment: "In a lawsuit the first to speak seems right, until someone comes forward and cross-examines" (Proverbs 18:17). We must also read between the lines in our personal lives when choosing potential partners. We are warned in Proverbs that "the lips of the adulterous woman drip honey, and her speech is smoother than oil; but in the end she is bitter as gall, sharp as a double-edged sword. Her feet go down to death; her steps lead straight to the grave" (Proverbs 5:3–5). Our goal is to discern substance from smooth talk.

The Dark Side of Praise

"What do you want?" we ask the coworker who is buttering us up at the office, probably about to ask us to help them move or donate toward their child's fundraiser. Although we are probably joking, we pose an excellent question. Genuine compliments are graciously received, but insincerity is suspect.

When someone has focused their attention on us, the important question to ask ourselves is *why*. By recognizing the seduction of selective attention and the allure of affirmation, we're equipped to separate honest friends from those who use flattery to set a trap, as Proverbs 29:5 warns: "Those who flatter their neighbors are spreading nets for their feet." And Paul appeals to his readers to be alert and watchful for divisive people who are not serving the Lord but their "own appetites," deceiving the minds of the naïve through "smooth talk and flattery" (Romans 16:17–18).

> When someone has focused their attention on us,
> the important question to ask ourselves is *why*.

Beyond flattery, smooth words reveal the soul of the speaker in other ways too. Venom is sometimes lined with velvet. Some of the most insensitive, demeaning, insulting sentiments come in a soft shell. Subtle swords of spite are weapons in the toolbox of the friend who asks, "You are not really going to wear that to the party, are you?" or "Don't you think you are too old to talk like that?" Some people are subjected to thinly veiled disdain in the workplace, like from a supervisor who condescendingly offers the observation, "You do a really good job when you concentrate."

In all of these examples, motivation matters, as does context—public or private. But content is important, too, as Paul advises us to avoid unwholesome talk and focus only on "what is helpful for building others up according to their needs, that it may benefit those who listen" (Ephesians 4:29). He cautions us to avoid "anger, rage, malice, slander, and filthy language" (Colossians 3:8), noting there should be no "obscenity, foolish talk or coarse joking, which are out of place, but rather thanksgiving" (Ephesians 5:4).

One of the best ways to avoid being seduced by a silver tongue is to both look and listen because attention is perception.

Verbal Accountability

In contrast to false flattery, authentic people speak the truth at all times, even if it is something you do not want to hear. Proverbs reads that "Wounds from a friend can be trusted, but an enemy multiplies kisses" (27:6). True friends are committed to speaking truth, and "pleasantness...springs from their heartfelt advice" (v. 9).

Yet when it comes to words, more is not necessarily better. Jesus instructs, "When you pray, do not keep on babbling like pagans, for they think they will be heard because of their many words" (Matthew 6:7). On the other hand, the apostle Paul shared the truth of Christ all night long (see Acts 20:11). The difference is the content. A person who likes to talk may be sharing pearls of wisdom or might just be a windbag: "Fools find no pleasure in understanding but delight in airing their own opinions" (Proverbs 18:2). Of course, healthy discussion benefits everyone, but no one is enlightened by longwinded chatterbox.

In stark contrast to the "say anything" approach that many educators adopt today in which there's no such thing as a bad idea, biblical teaching is revered as something to be taken seriously: "Not many of you should become teachers, my fellow believers, because you know that we who teach will be judged more strictly" (James 3:1). And not all "religious" teaching is biblical; some ideas are heretical.

We discern sound teaching through the extent to which it is based on Scripture, not social climate. The former is sound and sturdy; the latter changes like the wind based on trends. Listen carefully.

CHAPTER 5

WHEN YOU HEAR WHAT YOU WANT TO HEAR

To suit their own desires, they will gather around them a great number of teachers to say what their itching ears want to hear.
2 Timothy 4:3

Most people listen to friends, flames, and family through a filter of favoritism. And when someone we like is talking, we may engage in selective listening. In other words, we hear what we want to hear. Sweet nothings are pleasant, loving, and flattering but all-too-often untrue. In a group, for example, let's say you exchange charming, pleasant conversation with someone who leaves you feeling enamored by them, but the person standing right next to you who isn't charmed by that same person might experience the conversation completely differently.

Conversely, when someone makes uncomfortable, offensive, or alarming statements, some people discount them: "Oh, she's just talking; she doesn't mean that…That's just my brother… Don't pay any attention to what he said; they're just words." But words are often followed by action. When threat assessment professionals are evaluating potential danger, leakage refers to the communication of an intention to do harm. As I mentioned in chapter one, many mass shooters talked about their massacres before committing them and often to multiple people. We need to listen carefully when people talk.

The Art of Listening

Considering that lawyers talk for a living, it's ironic that one of the biggest, most common mistakes we make in the courtroom is failing to listen. When lawyers are tied to a "script" when questioning a witness, they miss significant opportunities for follow-up. The same is true on a first date, where each party is so intent on making a good impression that they miss chances to explore the golden nuggets of revealing information that they're receiving. But unlike a witness examination, narrowly tailored to specific facts, anything is on the menu at a first meeting with a prospective paramour. Pay attention to what your dinner dates choose to discuss.

When attempting to understand what went wrong in a failed relationship, we often look in the rearview mirror and rewind the tape. Sometimes, we're able to pinpoint early disclosures that were red flags in retrospect. Or maybe after your breakup, a friend or family member reminds you, "Don't you remember what he said?" Chances are, you were too busy looking instead of listening, or you fell victim to selective listening, only listening to the parts you wanted to hear. Even if we are blinded by a speaker's good looks, that does not mean that we must also become deaf to our concerns about them.

Judging Character through Conversation

Maria[1] is approached by a handsome new hire in the company lunchroom. Enamored with his wavy black hair and dimples, she listens raptly as he introduces himself and shares his background. Although the topics are innocent enough at the beginning—job history and hometown—as they continue to talk, he begins to mention his extracurricular activities, including drinking and gambling. Then he begins to sprinkle in profanity.

Maria disregards his after-hours references, assuming that many men drink and gamble, and she discounts his vulgar language, some of which is degrading toward women, rationalizing that many people talk that way even though she does not. If the conversation ends with a proposed coffee date, should Maria accept?

If you are in a situation where everyone is supposed to be on their best behavior and someone talks about inappropriate subjects, or if someone lets profanity fly when they first meet you, fasten your seatbelt because you are in for a turbulent ride with them should a relationship of any kind ever get off the ground.

* Note that I'll use the name Maria throughout this book in illustrative scenarios.

A gracious explanation for inappropriate or coarse language could be background, culture, prior workplace climate, or upbringing. Old habits die hard, and manners evolve over time. But in terms of topics, listening is learning. A striking set of expressive eyes may be windows to the soul, but words are windows to the heart.

The Revealing Nature of Words

The late Jeffrey Epstein, a convicted sex offender who died in his jail cell while facing federal charges for the sex trafficking of minors, reportedly admitted that he liked "young girls," as opposed to "young women"—a distinction noted by a *Vanity Fair* columnist who had seen Epstein on his private plane accompanied by several model-looking teenagers.[1] In retrospect, this was a distinction with a difference.

We are reminded that "out of the heart come evil thoughts—murder, adultery, sexual immorality, theft, false testimony, slander" (Matthew 15:19). Someone who talks favorably about unwholesome pursuits, jokes about past infidelity, or sticks up for sexual harassers or other types of lawbreakers is revealing the state of their heart and their moral compass.

Sometimes, character is revealed through what is left unsaid. Some people do not openly acknowledge their true beliefs because they love praise from others more than praise from God (see John 12:42–43). When they see injustice or mistreatment of others, some are unwilling to speak up out of fear of rocking the boat. Sexual misconduct and harassment thrive in settings where bystanders are unwilling to intervene. Silence is not golden when it emboldens perpetrators to continue their harmful behavior unchecked.

Words Are Weapons

Biblical knowledge arms you for spiritual battle. After all, the "sword of the Spirit" is the Word of God, a weapon of protection against evil (see Ephesians 6:10–17). Tragically, words are wielded as very different types of weapons in our world. In a society where, all too frequently, guns kill people, words kill people too.

You may remember the childhood chant, "Sticks and stones may break my bones, but words will never hurt me." Fact check: this is false. Cyberbullying, harassment, and other forms of public shaming can be devastating to vulnerable victims, sometimes leading to suicide. You may remember the conviction of Michelle Carter in 2017 for involuntary manslaughter in the infamous "texting suicide case," in which Carter persuaded her teenage boyfriend to take his own life.[2] From bullies to blackmailers, words can be deadly.

The tongue is aptly described as a small member of the body, able to create a forest fire with a small spark (see James 3:5). James 3:6 continues: "The tongue also is a fire, a world of evil among the parts of the body. It corrupts the whole body, sets the whole course of one's life on fire, and is itself set on fire by hell." Anyone who has experienced the trauma of a brutal argument or vicious verbal attack can attest to this truth.

Some garrulous individuals gravitate toward settings where they can engage in an ongoing war of words. Many law students and lawyers are stimulated by feisty discussion and debate, from the classroom to the courtroom. Having spent my entire adult life in this arena, I can share that the challenge is to separate those who argue for a living from those who live to argue. Because what might be considered a win in a courtroom may be a loss in your living room, where you just might win the argument but lose the war.

> What might be considered a win in a courtroom may be a loss in your living room, where you just might win the argument but lose the war.

So when you hear someone cue up a contrary viewpoint with phrases like, "For the sake of argument" or "Let me play devil's advocate," carefully consider what comes next. We are advised to "avoid foolish controversies and genealogies and arguments and quarrels about the law" because such activities are "unprofitable and useless" (Titus 3:9). We are reminded that "the Lord's servant must not be quarrelsome but must be kind to everyone, able to teach, not resentful" (2 Timothy 2:24). There is no need to speak harshly, as "a gentle tongue can break a bone" (Proverbs 25:15). We are instructed to do all things "without grumbling or arguing" (Philippians 2:14). You will always benefit by choosing reconciliation over conflict: "Blessed are the peace-makers, for they will be called children of God" (Matthew 5:9).

If someone consistently wants to disagree merely for the sake of argument, your time may be better spent elsewhere. Heed the wisdom of Titus 3:10: "Warn a divisive person once, and then warn them a second time. After that, have nothing to do with them."

CHAPTER 6

THE HALO OF HYPOCRISY

They claim to know God,
but by their actions they deny him.
TITUS 1:16

"Mind the gap" was an automated warning on public transportation in the United Kingdom that I became accustomed to hearing when I spent considerable time there both during law school and in seeking my doctorate degree. It is also good advice when it comes to learning about other people. That is, mind the gap between what people say and what they do.

Hypocrites often sound and look good. Really good. They boast about their virtuous behavior, appear respectable, and publicly engage in righteous deeds. But when judging a person's sincerity, appearances can be deceiving. Jesus referred to the teachers of the law and the Pharisees as beautiful on the outside but unclean on the inside, appearing as righteous but "full of hypocrisy and wickedness" (Matthew 23:27–28). He described their public behavior: "Everything they do is done for people to see: They make their phylacteries wide and the tassels on their garments long; they love the place of honor at banquets and the most important seats in the synagogues" (vv. 5–6). He warned us to heed their words but not emulate their behavior because they fail to practice what they preach (see v. 3). Hypocrisy was just as rampant in the times of the Old Testament, when people sat to hear God's Word but failed to put it into practice.

You may have heard some version of the saying: "The rules are for thee but not for me," as many people seem to espouse an attitude of "Do as I say, not as I do." Yet Scripture reminds us, "You…have no excuse, you who pass judgment on someone else, for at whatever point you judge another, you are condemning yourself, because you who pass judgment do the same things" (Romans 2:1). Again, listen to what people say but also take notice of what they do.

Show Me the Evidence

Talk is cheap. In court, it's not enough to tell a jury what happened in a particular case. As a prosecutor, I have to prove it by corroborating my assertions with evidence. This should be true outside the courtroom as well, yet some people are quick to believe everything they hear, especially when what they hear sounds appealing or supports their preexisting beliefs.

If you want to know what someone is truly like, watch what they do. Consider whether a person's talk matches their walk. The Bible warns us about rebellious people "full of meaningless talk and deception" who "claim to know God, but by their actions they deny him" (Titus 1:10, 16). They claim to know him but do not keep his commands (see 1 John 2:3–4).

Scripture advises us to display our character through conduct, to live such good lives that even pagans who accuse us of wrongdoing "may see your good deeds and glorify God" (1 Peter 2:12) and to let our light "shine before others" that they may view our good deeds and glorify God (Matthew 5:16), not us.

Actions Speak Louder Than Words

I have spent time inside a prison myself, arguing in front of the board of parole against a particular inmate's release. These kinds of hearings take place in a special room at the prison, and the inmates have a full opportunity to explain how they have reformed, what they have learned, and why it is now safe to release them. Some of these articulate lawbreakers can smooth talk their way through a parole hearing, but the real question is whether society will be safe if they return to the general population.

My job is to help the board answer that question by reviewing what the inmates have done during their period of confinement. Sometimes, the answer is that they've done nothing. Other times, it is worse. An inmate whose institutional behavior behind bars reveals a steady string of rule violations, acts of

insubordination, and a failure to participate in any type of reha-
bilitative classes or educational programs will contradict their
own assertions that they are reformed and ready to be released.
This phenomenon echoes the words of Matthew 12:35: "A good
man brings good things out of the good stored up in him, and an
evil man brings evil things out of the evil stored up in him." We
can even know children by their actions (see Proverbs 20:11).

Separating Sincere from Sanctimonious

A well-respected businesswoman visits the homeless every week
to personally deliver food and water. She volunteers at a local
domestic violence shelter, helping residents with their résumés.
She has been embezzling thousands of dollars from her company
for years. What is wrong with this picture? Could a seemingly
selfless humanitarian be capable of such a thing? Many jurors
will say no; it must be a mistake. It wasn't. This thief hid her true
motivation behind a cloak of credibility. Her compassion was a
costume, and her professed generosity was grandstanding.

We often fail to recognize hypocrites when we meet them
because we forget that when it comes to behavior, motive matters. Sex offender Jeffrey Epstein hid his deviant proclivities
behind a façade of philanthropy. His charitable foundation,
The Jeffrey Epstein VI Foundation, donated $30 million to
Harvard University in 2003 to establish a program in "mathe-
matical biology and evolutionary dynamics."[3] Infamous mobster
Al Capone, "Public Enemy Number One," ran a soup kitchen

in his community, providing free hot meals during the Great Depression.[4] Serial killer Ted Bundy was enrolled in a crime-prevention task force and worked at a suicide-prevention hotline when he was in college.[5] Clearly, outward acts of charity and compassion do not predict character.

Jesus noted that hypocrites "love to pray standing in the synagogues and on the street corners to be seen by others" (Matthew 6:5) and "disfigure their faces to show others they are fasting" (v. 16). But we are not to practice our righteousness in order to be seen. We are instructed that when we give to the needy, "do not announce it with trumpets, as the hypocrites do in the synagogues and on the streets, to be honored by others," but give in secret to be rewarded by God (vv. 1–4).

Jesus explained, "Not everyone who says to me, 'Lord, Lord,' will enter the kingdom of heaven, but only the one who does the will of my Father who is in heaven." He goes on to predict, "Many will say to me on that day, 'Lord, Lord, did we not prophesy in your name and in your name drive out demons and in your name perform many miracles?' Then I will tell them plainly, 'I never knew you. Away from me, you evildoers!'" (7:21–23).

Reality Revealed through Relationships

Authentic attention to the needs of others requires speaking and acting in love. That's why anonymous donors are often the most genuine, as are those who intentionally place others above themselves. As Romans reads, "We who are strong ought to bear with the failings of the weak and not to please ourselves. Each of us should please our neighbors for their good, to build them up" (15:1–2). But even the kindest words can be mere noise. Remember that "anyone who claims to be in the light but hates a brother or sister is still in the darkness" (1 John 2:9).

We also recognize that the way someone treats others predicts how they will treat us. A new paramour will not be on his or her best behavior forever, so whether speaking to a server on a first date or a ticket vendor at a ball game, we get a sneak preview of how they will treat us in the future.

The way someone treats others predicts how they will treat us.

Also consider the relationship someone has with his or her parents. Not only is the instruction to honor your father and mother one of the Ten Commandments (see Exodus 20:12), but it is also one of the most revealing aspects of a person's character and disposition. Jesus specifically cited this command in condemning the practice of declaring as devoted to God what should be used to help one's parents, elevating human tradition over God's commands (see Mark 7:9–12). And despite an outward profession of religiosity, Paul reminds us that "anyone who does not provide for their relatives, and especially for their own household, has denied the faith and is worse than an unbeliever" (1 Timothy 5:8). Proverbs even includes four-legged family members, noting that "the righteous care for the needs of their animals" (12:10).

We can also examine a person's relationship with extended family, meaning other people: "Do not rebuke an older man harshly, but exhort him as if he were your father. Treat younger men as brothers, older women as mothers, and younger women as sisters, with absolute purity" (1 Timothy 5:1–2).

But in evaluating someone's personal relationships, remember that it is easy to love those who love us (see Luke 6:32). Consider instead how people treat their enemies. Do they abide by the words found in Luke chapter 6?

> Love your enemies, do good to those who hate you, bless those who curse you, pray for those who mistreat you. If someone slaps you on one cheek, turn to them the other also. If someone takes your coat, do not withhold your shirt from them. Give to everyone who asks you, and if anyone takes what belongs to you, do not demand it back. Do to others as you would have them do to you. (vv. 27–31)

This last verse, known as the Golden Rule, is widely quoted in our world today. Treat others the way you want to be treated. It is a great way to show other people who you truly are and a good way to learn valuable information about others.

CHAPTER 7

THE FALLACY OF FEELINGS

The heart is deceitful above all things and beyond cure.
Who can understand it?
JEREMIAH 17:9

"Because of the way he made me feel" is an explanation often heard from crime victims when explaining why they became involved with a defendant. They believed him or her to be someone else, sometimes literally when in the case of manipulation through purposeful misidentification. When the criminal exposes his or her true colors, the betrayal is usually heart-breaking. Victims lament having missed so many red flags, often so brightly visible in retrospect. Yet the jurors who are examining the evidence through an objective lens struggle to understand how and why.

Feeling is believing. If we find someone appealing because of how they make us feel, then our attraction is based on chemistry, not compatibility. Feelings, not facts. If they make us feel unworthy or unimportant, we avoid them like the plague. If they make us feel desirable and valuable, we want them around as much as possible. To avoid being fooled, we must learn to distinguish authentic admiration from false manipulation.

> If we find someone appealing because of how they make us feel, then our attraction is based on chemistry, not compatibility.

When Superficial Seems Sincere

False feelings are faked, sometimes convincingly. Some child molesters marry "for show" to avoid suspicion. One of the hallmarks of such pairings is a husband's consistent verbal professions of adoration toward his wife, particularly in the absence of actions that support his claim. I have had numerous wives of child predators testify on behalf of their husbands, describing these men as loyal, faithful, and dedicated to their marriage.

Yet to an outside observer, behavioral evidence of such commitment is invisible. You might see one of these couples out to dinner, where a doting wife is attempting to catch the eye of her distant husband, whose attention is clearly focused elsewhere—often on children sitting at other tables. This couple won't be sharing a candlelit table in a quiet restaurant but more likely sharing a pizza at a noisy, family-oriented establishment filled with rambunctious youngsters.

A different dysfunctional dynamic characterizes marriages of convenience, which often masquerade as matches made in heaven. We assume two people are perfect for each other because they have similar interests and never fight. That may be because they did not marry for love. Power couples are often exactly that—without more. They enjoy the career opportunities that their union brings but never mix their business with pleasure. They do not get jealous or have personal disagreements, only professional differences. Watching them converse over a Caesar salad at a local steak house, you might assume you were observing a business lunch—because you are.

Godly relationships, in contrast, are emotional in nature. God is jealous for our attention because he loves us (see Exodus 20:4–5; 34:14; Deuteronomy 6:15). Spouses and partners feel jealous when other things compete for the attention of their significant other, yet not all passion is healthy or helpful.

The Wrong Kind of Passion

Smart women sometimes make bad choices. One of King David's wives, Abigail, whom he did not take as a wife until her husband died, was "an intelligent and beautiful woman," while her husband was "surly and mean" (1 Samuel 25:3). It's a notorious relational mismatch important enough to be recorded biblically. We know couples like this in our own lives and ask ourselves how such a pairing could have happened. While we don't know how it happened with Abigail, I can tell you exactly how it happens in many of the cases I have handled: progressively and predictably.

As a career sex crimes prosecutor, I am intimately familiar with how so-called exciting and passionate relationships become coercive and abusive. First of all, listening to victims describe the relational dynamics, I would not agree that it began as exciting and passionate but more like explosive and antagonistic. And inevitably, bad behavior gets worse. This progression does not occur overnight; it is a gradual process with plenty of red flags along the way.

Abusive individuals use emotion as a weapon to exert control over their victims. This is facilitated when the partners misidentify and glamorize negative emotions. Anger looks passionate, aggressive looks assertive, and rude looks honest. Jealousy can masquerade as love and possession as protection, causing red flags to look red hot. Many relationships become harmful both emotionally and physically when victims come to believe their partner's fixation or obsession reflects their love and devotion.

For some victims, toxic appears tolerable because they grew up believing they were unworthy of love and respect. Others have never experienced a healthy relationship and subsequently lack any type of model or comparison. They may view their partner as the best choice from a selection of other negative alternatives. Many victims compartmentalize the abuse, describing their partners as "good fathers" or "decent providers" determined to do the best they can. Unfortunately, sugarcoating maladaptive personality traits to make them tolerable leads to disappointment, dissatisfaction, and potential danger.

When Coercive Feels Consensual

Some relationships are driven by lust, not love. Many of these involve sexual coercion, where abusers pressure reluctant victims for intimacy, too much too soon. This can include pressuring partners into taking nude photos or videos or engaging in sexting. Some perpetrators engaging in sexual coercion escalate to sexual assault, feeling "entitled" to an increased amount of physical contact after a certain amount of courtship.

Coercive behavior is not an expression of love. Quite to the contrary, in fact. Yet research reveals that sexual coercion is more common within long-term intimate relationships than casual relationships.[6] This is partly because women have invested so much time into the relationship that they become reluctant to establish boundaries regarding sexual intimacy. Violence is not a necessary component of sexual coercion for it to create damaging feelings, such as sadness, guilt, and self-blame. In addition to negative emotional consequences, women may also engage in justification and minimization.[7] Many women maintain their relationships by intentionally mischaracterizing the abuse. They anticipate that the stigma, humiliation, and embarrassment of reporting the violative nature of the relationship might be more traumatic than enduring it. They attempt to resolve these feelings by telling themselves that the intimate activities are consensual and therefore acceptable. Of course, men experience sexual coercion too. However, far more often than not, it's women who fall victim to it.

When Enabling Feels like Empathy

As caring human beings, it feels good to display concern for each other when things go wrong. Especially when interacting with those less fortunate, we enjoy the feeling that comes with investing in people we feel sorry for—sometimes notwithstanding the callous way they might treat us or what they have done to others. But acting out of perceived obligation or sympathy is not a productive path to follow. As many children learn, it is physically easier to pull someone down than to pull someone up. The same is true emotionally.

Many community organizations target at-risk youth and adults in attempts to improve their lives. Sometimes the result is successful but not always, despite the best of intentions. Optimism alone isn't enough. Some people see others as projects and believe if they just work hard enough, then they can transform a bad person into a good person. Human nature leads some people to continue to believe someone can be reformed despite consistent evidence to the contrary. Some friends and neighbors of convicted child molesters proclaim that notwithstanding their knowledge of multiple victims, they would still allow the defendant to babysit their kids.

When confronted with professional misbehavior, we might feel obligated to grant a person of prestige the benefit of the doubt or chalk our observations up to the assumption that a certain behavior is out of character. Unfortunately, the bad behavior we see may very well be a distinct, clear expression of character.

Many domestic violence victims mischaracterize their partner's abuse as "acting out" or "expressing frustration," justifying such behavior on a perpetrator's bad childhood, pressure at work, or drugs or alcohol. Misplaced empathy allows victims to deny, diminish, and defend dangerous behavior, sometimes with disastrous or deadly consequences.

Live by Faith, Not Feelings

Instead of following your feelings, consider biblical wisdom that promotes emotional management: "Whoever is patient has great understanding, but one who is quick-tempered displays folly" (Proverbs 14:29). We are warned not to be "quickly provoked," because "anger resides in the lap of fools" (Ecclesiastes 7:9) but instead to manage our emotions: "A gentle answer turns away wrath, but a harsh word stirs up anger" (Proverbs 15:1). A wise person resists becoming angry even when provoked, as "wisdom yields patience; it is to one's glory to overlook an offense" (19:11).

Sometimes the root of our emotions is elusive. For example, have you ever been in a meeting or at a gathering and suddenly felt anxious when a certain person walked into the room? *I didn't know he was coming*, you might think to yourself, now feeling uncomfortable. Your visceral reaction and quick change in mood might stem from the way this person has treated you in the past. Or your response might not have to do with the person at all but someone he or she reminds you of. Either way, you have been triggered. But can you trust your feelings?

Frequently, we mask, muffle, misinterpret, discount, or disregard our feelings—even when they should serve as an early signal from our internal warning system. Faith is a stronger and more reliable basis for assessing situations and making decisions, especially ones that create uncertainty and anxiety. Scripture encourages us to be anxious for nothing but instead, through prayer and petition and with thankfulness, to present our requests to God, whose peace "transcends all understanding" and will guard our hearts and minds (Philippians 4:6–7).

Whether professionally or personally, when we are not at peace, our conscience is speaking. But we need biblical wisdom to interpret and understand the message. If you make decisions in life and love based merely on feelings, then you will fail to take the necessary steps to protect yourself from dangerous people and toxic relationships, and you will miss out on the rewarding relationships you could have if you live by faith.

CHAPTER 8

WHEN BAD FEELS GOOD

The eye never has enough of seeing,
nor the ear its fill of hearing.
ECCLESIASTES 1:8

Physically or emotionally, through social contact or substance use, positive feelings drive proactive behavior designed to seek and maintain a high. There are plenty of natural, healthy, dopamine-releasing methods of feeling good—from exercise to music to falling in love. But there is also a tipping point at which use becomes abuse and focus becomes fixation. People become addicted to people or activities in the same way they might become hooked on drugs or alcohol. And when attention becomes obsession, socializing can turn into stalking. So if the problem is too much of a good thing, why is it so difficult to draw the line?

Peter describes the pagan lifestyle as "debauchery, lust, drunkenness, orgies, carousing and detestable idolatry" (1 Peter 4:3). But most people would not relate to those extremes. They experience romantic attraction, enjoy a glass of wine with dinner, and have a variety of worldly goals, financially, socially, and physically. So the question is, when does sensuality become sin?

Often, the answer is when an activity or urge is prideful and predominantly self-centered. Paul describes enemies of Christ as destined for destruction because "their god is their stomach, and their glory is in their shame" (Philippians 3:18–19). One of the hallmarks of the "terrible times" in the last days is people becoming "lovers of pleasure rather than lovers of God" (2 Timothy 3:4). We should be intentional about recognizing the difference because the Bible instructs us to "clothe [ourselves] with the Lord Jesus Christ, and do not think about how to gratify the desires of the flesh" (Romans 13:14).

Flash over Substance

Smart advertising sells both the steak and the sizzle. Because consumers have an appetite for sensual pleasure and short attention spans, we are attuned to sales pitches about how a product or service will make us more beautiful, smarter, and richer or how it promises to make us feel powerful, happy, and desirable. Advertisers know that human eyes are never satisfied, "for everything in the world—the lust of the flesh, the lust of the eyes, and the pride of life—comes not from the Father but from the world" (1 John 2:16).

But as I taught my upper division business ethics students for years, savvy shoppers know that what they see is not necessarily what they will get. Whether buying a new phone or a new car, beware the bait and switch. We are deceived by false promises made by famous people, from cultural icons to celebrities, many of whom have never used the very product they are promoting.

Eve fell victim to strategic, deceptive marketing in the garden of Eden when she bit the apple. Although it was forbidden fruit, it was pleasing to the eye, appeared to be good for food, and desirable for attaining wisdom (see Genesis 3:6). The false advertiser was the serpent, described in Genesis 3:1 as "more crafty" than any of the other animals God made. After Eve disobeyed God's instruction not to eat from the forbidden tree, she shared the fruit with Adam, and we have been in danger ever since.

Paul warned the Corinthians, "I am afraid that just as Eve was deceived by the serpent's cunning, your minds may somehow be led astray from your sincere and pure devotion to Christ" (2 Corinthians 11:3). Paul's fear was well-founded. Deception through flattery, flash, and false promises is predictable and preventable if you are paying attention.

Too Much of a Good Thing

Many people look forward to a drink at the end of a long day. Some people have an occasional glass of wine with dinner. But for people who cannot stop at one glass, the experience of pleasure turns into misfortune and regret. King Solomon warns that "it is not for kings to drink wine, not for rulers to crave beer, lest they drink and forget what has been decreed, and deprive all the oppressed of their rights" (Proverbs 31:4–5). He explains that as inviting as wine looks as it "sparkles in the cup" and "goes down smoothly," afterward, we will "see strange sights" and "imagine confusing things" (23:31–33). "Woe to those who are heroes at drinking wine and champions at mixing drinks" (Isaiah 5:22).

There can be too much of a good thing. As Proverbs reads, "Wine is a mocker and beer a brawler; whoever is led astray by them is not wise" (20:1). Notice the emphasis on being led astray. The condemnation is not about food and wine but gluttony and drunkenness (see 23:20–21). And there is more at stake than experiencing a hangover or food coma: "Drunkards and gluttons become poor, and drowsiness clothes them in rags" (v. 21). Ultimately, overindulgence will compromise both good health and good judgment.

As a sex crimes prosecutor, I have seen overindulgence make people vulnerable to prurient and voyeuristic manipulation. It's reminiscent of a warning from Habakkuk: "Woe to him who gives drink to his neighbors, pouring it from the wineskin till they are drunk, so that he can gaze on their naked bodies!"

(2:15). We are instead instructed to "behave decently, as in the daytime, not in carousing and drunkenness, not in sexual immorality and debauchery" (Romans 13:13). Paul describes debauchery and drunkenness as "acts of the flesh" (Galatians 5:19–21). Often paired together, Paul also specifically advises, "Do not get drunk on wine, which leads to debauchery. Instead, be filled with the Spirit" (Ephesians 5:18).

Clearly, most people do not spend their free time carousing in orgies or drunkenness. But we are advised to avoid overindulgence of any kind. We strive to live in moderation, remembering that our bodies are temples of God (see 1 Corinthians 6:19), which we are to present as a living sacrifice (see Romans 12:1). We strengthen our resolve by walking by the Spirit in order to avoid gratifying the "desires of the flesh" (Galatians 5:16), remembering that "man does not live on bread alone but on every word that comes from the mouth of the LORD" (Deuteronomy 8:3). "So whether you eat or drink or whatever you do, do it all for the glory of God" (1 Corinthians 10:31).

When Good Feels Good

The Bible doesn't teach that *everything* that feels good is a sin. It does not instruct us to live a solitary life, destitute and deprived. On the contrary, Scripture encourages us and God designed us to live, laugh, and love in community. "A cheerful heart is good medicine" (Proverbs 17:22). Biblical warnings about sensual pleasures and temptations are designed to preserve and protect, not punish.

King Solomon advises that the gift of God is to eat, drink, and find satisfaction in our work (see Ecclesiastes 3:13). We are not directed toward deprivation but moderation: "If you find honey, eat just enough" (Proverbs 25:16). And Proverbs further reminds us that temperance requires restraint. "When you sit to dine with a ruler, note well what is before you," and take preventative measures if you are inclined toward gluttony (23:1–2).

> Biblical warnings about sensual pleasures and temptations are designed to preserve and protect, not punish.

In discussing mistaken beliefs about eating food sacrificed to idols, Paul notes that "food does not bring us near to God; we are no worse if we do not eat, and no better if we do" (1 Corinthians 8:8). Yet he recognizes the potential for adversely influencing others by example, vowing that "if what I eat causes my brother or sister to fall into sin, I will never eat meat again, so that I will not cause them to fall" (v. 13).

There is no biblical prohibition over feeling good and experiencing pleasure. On the contrary, God's plan is to inspire us to find permanent peace and comfort instead of chasing cheap thrills and fleshly indulgence. "Take delight in the LORD, and he will give you the desires of your heart" (Psalm 37:4).

CHAPTER 9

WHEN HASTE MAKES WASTE

Desire without knowledge is not good—
how much more will hasty feet miss the way!
PROVERBS 19:2

We all know the dangers of grocery shopping when we are hungry, and yet it doesn't always stop us. It's an easy but bad habit to develop because we live in a society of instant gratification, where we can buy almost anything we want with a tap on our smartphone at any time of the day or night—often without doing the prior research necessary to make an informed choice. Once our order arrives and our pupils dilate, feasting our eyes on our latest purchase, only prudent consumers are able to ration wisely: "The wise store up choice food and olive oil, but fools gulp theirs down" (Proverbs 21:20).

People indulge too quickly and too soon when in the market for a relationship as well, becoming involved with the wrong person for the wrong reasons at the wrong time. Whether on the rebound or racing the biological clock, some women sprint down the aisle with a relational mismatch, abandoning plans to find "Mr. Right" and settling for "Mr. Right Now."

This phenomenon of settling may actually change the perception and behavior of bar patrons looking to partner up. Research indicates that when prospects are dwindling as the hour gets later, potential partners are perceived as better looking.[8] Advertising and marketing use this "last call" phenomenon as well.

When a product is showcased as "limited edition" or only "one left at this price" and then paired with information about how many other people want it, consumers are more likely to perceive that thing as more attractive than it actually is. This is also why television offers often come with a time limit and free gifts thrown in if you buy a product within the next ten minutes. Advertisers know that if you cool off and allow yourself to replace emotion with logic, then you will probably realize that you don't need it or can buy it elsewhere for less: "Like a city whose walls are broken through is a person who lacks self-control" (Proverbs 25:28).

We strive to develop our faith, incorporating characteristics such as goodness, knowledge, and self-control (see 2 Peter 1:5–6). Resisting impulsivity prevents you from settling for less so that God can deliver something better.

Resisting impulsivity prevents you from settling for less so that God can deliver something better.

The Comfort of Contentment

Speaking of shopping when you are hungry, you will also want to avoid making important decisions when you are hungry, both literally and figuratively. The book of Genesis details the story of brothers Jacob and Esau and how Esau, the eldest, sold his birthright to Jacob for a bowl of stew because he was famished (see Genesis 25:29–34).

We can take a lesson from Esau when we are feeling desperate to fulfill some type of need, as biblical contentment does not depend on circumstances. We can learn to be content in every situation, "whether well fed or hungry, whether living in plenty or in want" (Philippians 4:12). The ability to identify our state of mind is an important learned skill, and practicing contentment as a spiritual discipline is a blueprint for peace. God does not promise instant gratification but instead reveals the "path of life" and fills us with joy and "eternal pleasures" (Psalm 16:11).

Timing matters too. With discernment, you can distinguish between what looks good and what is good, including what is good for you and when. When we pray for something, God's answer may be yes, no, or wait. Not everyone can handle fame and fortune right out of college or a whirlwind relationship too soon after a breakup. As the old adage goes, good things come to those who wait. Other times, we thank God for unanswered prayers. But in both cases, patience is a virtue.

The Profitability of Patience

God's timing is perfect. "There is a time for everything, and a season for every activity under the heavens" (Ecclesiastes 3:1). Paul reminds us to be "joyful in hope, patient in affliction, faithful in prayer" (Romans 12:12). Elsewhere, he encourages us to persevere and "not become weary in doing good," assured that at the right time "we will reap a harvest if we do not give up" (Galatians 6:9). Scripture even calls upon us to exercise patience in suffering:

> Be patient, then, brothers and sisters, until the Lord's coming. See how the farmer waits for the land to yield its valuable crop, patiently waiting for the autumn and spring rains. You too, be patient and stand firm, because the Lord's coming is near. (James 5:7–8)

We can also observe patience in the way we approach relationships: "Love is patient, love is kind" (1 Corinthians 13:4). Scripture instructs us to "be completely humble and gentle; be patient, bearing with one another in love" (Ephesians 4:2) and reminds us, "as God's chosen people, holy and dearly loved," to clothe ourselves with "compassion, kindness, humility, gentleness and patience" (Colossians 3:12). Paul urged new believers to "warn those who are idle and disruptive, encourage the disheartened, help the weak, be patient with everyone" (1 Thessalonians 5:14). Patience is also practical in terms of personal credibility, as Proverbs reminds us that "through patience a ruler can be persuaded" (25:15).

Patience is also helpful when it seems like wrongdoers are getting ahead. Rest assured that they will get what they have coming:

> Be still before the LORD and wait patiently for him; do not fret when people succeed in their ways, when they carry out their wicked schemes. Refrain from anger and turn from wrath; do not fret—it leads only to evil. For those who are evil will be destroyed, but those who hope in the LORD will inherit the land. (Psalm 37:7–9)

Expand your perspective by substituting instant gratification with godly goals. Time and effort spent on prayerfully cultivating the ability to be satisfied in any circumstance is a blessing to us, as well as to others, because contentment is contagious. Be prepared not only to enjoy peace yourself but also to be praised as a patient peacemaker.

CHAPTER 10

THE ALLURE OF IDOLATRY

"You shall have no other gods before me."

EXODUS 20:3

The home of one of the stalkers I prosecuted appeared nondescript from the outside. Even the living room was unremarkable with simple furniture and a modest television set. But the suspect's bedroom told quite a different story. Covered with photographs and posters of the young female pop star that had become his obsession, it included an altar, complete with incense, candles, and a lock of the celebrity's hair that he paid dearly for in an online auction. True, most cases of idol worship are not this extreme, but they are identifiable.

The first of the Ten Commandments prohibits idolatry. Expanding on the prohibition of having any gods before the one true God, it states: "You shall not make for yourself an image in the form of anything in heaven above or on the earth beneath or in the waters below. You shall not bow down to them or worship them" (Exodus 20:4–5). Most people today don't have household objects they worship or physically bow down to. But idolatry encompasses more than that. It is subtle, pervasive, and insidious.

The editors of *Encyclopedia Britannica* define idolatry as "the worship of someone or something other than God as though it were God." This definition encompasses overt idolatry, which they define as "explicit acts of reverence addressed to a person or an object,"[9] such as a ruler, animal, statue of gold or bronze, or even the sun or moon. But an idol does not have to be a golden calf, as the rebellious nation made when Moses went up on the mountain to meet with God after he had led them out of Egypt (see Exodus 32). Worshiping creation instead of the Creator is one of the ways people have descended into all types of depravity (see Romans 1:25).

In many cases, people have met their downfall by idolizing what they have made. In a land of abundance filled with silver and gold, endless horses and chariots, "Their land is full of idols; they bow down to the work of their hands, to what their fingers have made. So people will be brought low and everyone humbled" (Isaiah 2:8–9). This is true even though we might recognize the futility of relying on manufactured goods: "Of what value is an idol carved by a craftsman? Or an image that teaches lies? For the one who makes it trusts in his own creation; he makes idols that cannot speak" (Habakkuk 2:18).

True, most people can relate to the senselessness of physical idols: "They say to wood, 'You are my father,' and to stone, 'You gave me birth'" (Jeremiah 2:27). The danger is becoming devoted to and blinded by worldly desires. Although idols made by human hands from silver and gold cannot see, hear, feel, walk, or talk, the Bible warns us that "those who make them will be like them, and so will all who trust in them" (Psalm 115:8).

Idolatry as worship, reverence, or devotion to something other than God can be manifest through a relationship, an addiction, a hobby, or even a vocation. Anything that takes the place of God in our lives can become an idol. Yet because worldly pursuits can appear to be admirable, alluring, and even enjoyable, the first step in addressing idolatry is identification.

Identifying Idolatry

Whether you toss a coin into a wishing well or envision a magic genie inside a lamp ready to hear your request, if you had one wish, what would it be? Popular answers include health and wealth or prosperity and popularity. Even if you would admirably use your wish to benefit a loved one, most people reveal their inner priorities and pursuits through outward prayers and petitions. There is nothing wrong with having goals and objectives; the problem arises with the focus and manner in which they are pursued: "No one can serve two masters. Either you will hate the one and love the other, or you will be devoted to the one and despise the other. You cannot serve both God and money" (Matthew 6:24).

Many people worship at an alter dedicated to something other than God. They are focused on materialism, wealth, self, or a desire for certain things or people. Some are addictions, such as drugs, alcohol, gambling, or pornography, as idolatry is described as a work of the flesh (see Galatians 5:19–21). "Their destiny is destruction, their god is their stomach, and their glory is in their shame. Their mind is set on earthly things" (Philippians 3:19).

Sometimes, idolatry involves interests that are not inherently harmful but dangerous when pursued to the exclusion of everything else. Workaholics often neglect family, friends, and even their own health in pursuit of wealth that they will never have the chance to enjoy. Fitness fanatics might experience the same narrow focus, neglecting family and even financial responsibility to maximize time spent chasing a favorite sport or idealized body.

The key is to be able to distinguish interest from idolatry. Some world travelers exhibit a passion for the exotic through their home décor, displaying artifacts and collectibles from around the globe. Others showcase goals and aspirations through an office "brag wall" full of awards, commendations, and photographs with politicians. But there comes a point when interest becomes obsession. Predictably, one of the hallmarks of idolatry, which others can easily recognize, is an unhealthy focus on self.

Worshiping at the Altar of Self

The second greatest commandment is to "love your neighbor as yourself" (Matthew 22:39), which assumes that we love ourselves. But self-love can become selfish. One of the signs of the "terrible times in the last days" will be people becoming "lovers of themselves" (2 Timothy 3:1–2). That characterizes many people today.

We are born selfish and, as we grow up, enjoy consuming and surrounding ourselves with anything that promotes our sense of self-esteem and self-confidence. Popular magazines capture our attention with titles like *Self, Us, People, Vogue, Glamour,* and *Good Housekeeping,* catering to our desire to improve our appearance, image, and surroundings.

Selfishness in the extreme produces some of the most disturbing cases I have prosecuted, from neglecting elders to disposing of newborn babies in dumpsters—many of whom are thankfully located and rescued by sharp-eared neighbors who hear their cries. Yet selfishness is not always manifest through criminal behavior but, often, a callous disregard for others.

You may have heard that the biblical concept of the Trinity is not "me, myself, and I." Instead, the Bible advises us, "Do nothing out of selfish ambition or vain conceit," but in humility, to value others over ourselves, prioritizing their interests over our own (Philippians 2:3–4). This should encourage us to appreciate the value of relationships instead of "looking out for number one" or asking, "What's in it for me?" And sure enough, as you have no doubt experienced in many different settings, we are happier and healthier when we focus on others instead of ourselves.

Choose Godly Ideals over Idols

Paul is direct and to the point in advising us to "flee from idolatry" (1 Corinthians 10:14), considering the grave warnings about the dangers of idolatry. "If you ever forget the LORD your God and follow other gods and worship and bow down to them, I testify against you today that you will surely be destroyed" (Deuteronomy 8:19).

Yet some people practice idolatry without even realizing it. Paul described this phenomenon as he observed it in Athens: "As I walked around and looked carefully at your objects of worship, I even found an altar with this inscription: TO AN UNKNOWN GOD. So you are ignorant of the very thing you worship" (Acts 17:23). We are wise to ask ourselves what we worship and why we desire the goals that we pursue. From relationships to reputation, income to image, money to marriage, motivation matters in order to walk with godly purpose instead of running like a rat on a wheel. As Romans reads, "The mind governed by the flesh is death, but the mind governed by the Spirit is life and peace" (8:6).

We are wise to ask ourselves what we worship and why we desire the goals that we pursue.

If we seek to walk by the Spirit, God will give us what we truly desire: "Take delight in the LORD, and he will give you the desires of your heart" (Psalm 37:4). And when we pursue the right goals, God will give us the strength to achieve them (see Philippians 4:13).

CHAPTER 11

WHEN LESS LOOKS LIKE MORE

As iron sharpens iron,
so one person sharpens another.
PROVERBS 27:17

Many people can remember the campus buzz around the "new girl" at school or the chatter about the "new kid on the block" in their neighborhood. Novelty is interesting, especially before we know too much about the newcomer. In fact, we are often interested *because* we don't know much about the newcomer. But we run into problems when we are attracted to novelty for its own sake, without more.

Some of the most notorious criminals have been able to infiltrate neighborhoods, communities, and workplaces by hardly leaving a trail, ensuring no one knew too much about them, which often made them interesting. Often described in retrospect as "nice," "pleasant," and "easygoing," they were able to interact superficially without drawing suspicion. Although everyone appreciates the value of getting to know others as relationships develop, dangerous people capitalize on the premise that, when it comes to initial attraction, sometimes less is more.

The Infatuation of Intrigue

Enamored by mystique, many people believe that ignorance is bliss. Masquerade balls and Halloween parties capitalize on the appeal of disguise. Concealment creates curiosity, which generates interest and intrigue. But in reality, this mindset can be dangerous.

As relationships develop, no one wants to reveal too much too soon. We should always leave certain things to the imagination—just not the important things. Yet within the throes of infatuation, some people revel in the belief that ignorance is bliss. The less you know about someone, the more you can use your imagination to fill in the details—favorably. Unfortunately, rose-colored glasses camouflage red flags.

For some people, uncertainty can heighten feelings of attraction. Feelings of butterflies in the stomach regularly occur during the romantic anticipation stage of a relationship, before couples know each other very well, creating a pleasurable sense of nervous excitement as mutual feelings develop.

But sometimes, what you don't know *can* hurt you. I have prosecuted men who led double lives. Not quite like James Bond, although some drove fast foreign cars. And certainly not like

Superman, although some looked like Clark Kent in court with their slick dark hair and black-framed spectacles—even when they had perfect vision. But one red flag these mysterious men had in common, which was significant in retrospect, was their insistence on private time. Time to "unwind in the man cave" is what they often told their wives or girlfriends. Time to commit crime was the real explanation in the cases I handled.

Sometimes, what you don't know *can* hurt you.

When Isolation Looks like Independence

Seeking time alone is not the problem. Even Jesus "often withdrew to lonely places and prayed" (Luke 5:16). And a married couple may mutually decide to separate briefly to devote themselves to prayer (see 1 Corinthians 7:5). But depending on the activity one desires to partake in, going dark can illuminate underlying motivation. A married man who enjoys bar hopping alone or maintains a separate address "to entertain" is displaying an unhealthy interest in guarding his independence and privacy. And not in a way that benefits his marriage.

In seeking time alone, there is a difference between introversion and isolation. Many good people live alone but remain connected to friends and family. Others completely withdraw from society. Unabomber Ted Kaczynski, a mathematics prodigy educated at Harvard and the University of Michigan, abandoned his academic career to live as a recluse in a secluded, remote wooded cabin with no electricity or running water, from where he embarked on a nationwide bombing campaign.

In the threat assessment world, although we often eschew the term for its deceivingly positive connotations, the concept of a "lone wolf" captures the misplaced sense of captivation others feel for mysterious suspects, which can hinder the reporting of suspicious behavior. Neighbors of the proverbial ax murderer next door, whom incredulous neighbors in retrospect describe as "such a nice guy" who kept to himself, often regret not having sought out more information about someone who lived so close.

But even if you know your next-door neighbor in the present, you should know something about their past. Because history impacts credibility, it is difficult to judge someone in the present who has no past. Some strangers seem sweet and vulnerable, out of place and out of touch. But bystander beware: sometimes friendly visitors are villains.

Less is not more when looking for individuals on the run from the law. The biggest challenge of prosecuting fugitives is finding them. We expect they have altered their appearance, seeking to deceive through disguise. But that might not be necessary because some locations are so remote and desolate that they are places people go to disappear. Research on sex offender fugitives reveals they were five times more likely to live alone than with others, even after controlling for other background and demographic factors.[10]

Thankfully, many secluded jurisdictions are tight-knit communities. If somebody shows up who appears to be a nobody from nowhere, a present without a past, people become suspicious. Can you imagine meeting someone without a smartphone cache of personal photos in a day and age where our devices are filled to capacity with photo galleries chronicling our lives and loved ones? Assuming someone is not in the witness protection program, someone who claims to have no history may indeed have a *criminal* history and deliberately hide their identity through anonymity.

People Are Better Together

We are not designed for a solitary existence. God created Eve for Adam, although he was living in the garden of paradise (see Genesis 2:18). King Solomon emphasizes the value of safety in numbers:

> Two are better than one, because they have a good return for their labor: If either of them falls down, one can help the other up. But pity anyone who falls and has no one to help them up. Also, if two lie down together, they will keep warm. But how can one keep warm alone? (Ecclesiastes 4:9–11)

In terms of unity as Christians, we are reminded that "the body does not consist of one member but of many" (1 Corinthians 12:14 ESV). "If one member suffers, all suffer together; if one member is honored, all rejoice together" (v. 26 ESV). We are designed to rely on each other and seek each other out for advice: "As iron sharpens iron, so one person sharpens another" (Proverbs 27:17). Godly friends and family can provide sturdy sounding boards of objectivity. The book of Proverbs supports seeking solid counsel, noting that without guidance, a nation falls, but an abundance of counselors provides victory (see 11:14) and that without counsel, plans fail, but they succeed with many advisers (see 15:22).

In both life and love, less is not more. Knowledge is power, information breeds intelligence, and safety is found in numbers. Replace the mystery of mystique with the comfort of consistency and companionship.

CHAPTER 12

WHEN RISKY LOOKS REWARDING

The prudent see danger and take refuge,
but the simple keep going and pay the penalty.
PROVERBS 22:3

Many people grow up with Tinseltown tales of dark heroes and motorcycle-riding bad boys, brave, bold, and brazen, inviting us to take a walk on the wild side. Handsome daredevils make dangerous look desirable, and the glamorized lifestyles of the foolish but famous influence many young people. But unfortunately, unlike the latest *James Bond* sensational stunt, in reality, the balance of risk and reward rarely tilts in favor of the risk-taker. Sensationalizing bad behavior only leads to bad decisions.

Sometimes, alluring behavior is not necessarily bad but dangerous. One example of this is extreme sports, where fans turn out in droves to watch daring athletes engage in nail-biting, death-defying stunts and fearless feats. Inspired by what they see, some people attempt to reproduce such stunts despite endless warnings that they should not try this at home.

Even for professionally trained athletes, who are in peak physical condition and take all of the precautions to prevent injury, extreme sports pose a level of danger. Motorcycle stunt legend Evel Knievel made the *Guinness Book of World Records* for "most bones broken in a lifetime," with 433 breaks during the course of his career.[11] But many people are drawn to the appreciation of danger itself. They walk tightropes between skyscrapers or "elevator surf" by standing on the tops of moving elevators, leaping from one car to the next. Extreme tourism caters to the allure of unnecessary experimentation or dangerous investigation. It is one thing to visit well-maintained, publicly accessible historical sites but quite another to visit the post-apocalyptic town of Chernobyl.

For other people, anything "off limits" is enticing simply for the thrill of breaking the rules. Trespassing into closed businesses or abandoned homes and exploring with flashlights, often memorializing the illegal excursions on video, appeals to people who never intend to steal. The enjoyment is the adventure and, often, royalties from posting the documentation. But such ill-intentioned escapades can lead to injuries from hidden hazards, including other trespassers or being caught and subsequently saddled with a criminal record.

Many prohibited activities come with posted warnings highlighting the present danger, like a red flag on the beach during high-surf conditions or signs indicating to swimmers that no lifeguard is on duty. Warnings are designed to protect people from their own curiosity.

When Curiosity Leads to Catastrophe

When I worked in juvenile court, I prosecuted young people for breaking into vacant structures and engaging in everything from theft to vandalism. Such "attractive nuisances," as they are often referred to in tort law, include swimming pools, animal enclosures, and all types of abandoned homes and businesses. These locations are dangerous magnets for curious youths, especially if someone has specifically warned them to steer clear. The parental mandate, "Whatever you do, don't go inside that building!" almost guarantees noncompliance.

Curiosity is a natural human state: "It is the glory of God to conceal a matter; to search out a matter is the glory of kings" (Proverbs 25:2). In other words, curiosity is not always a bad thing. Paul was able to share the good news about Jesus with a large audience in Athens because the residents "spent their time doing nothing but talking about and listening to the latest ideas" (Acts 17:21).

But curiosity can foster vulnerability. Child molesters prey upon the curiosity of children, exploiting the inquisitiveness of young minds. Many of my cases have involved trusted mentors and neighbors exposing adolescents to alcohol, drugs, or pornography. Parents are well warned to explore the types of activities that educators and role models are sharing with their children.

And some things are not meant for us to know. As Jesus explained to his disciples when they asked if he was going to restore the kingdom to Israel, "It is not for you to know the times or dates the Father has set by his own authority" (1:7). Or to Peter when he asked about the Lord's plan for John, "If I want him to remain alive until I return, what is that to you? You must follow me" (John 21:22).

In some cases, curiosity can be dangerous or even deadly. Accordingly, people sometimes must be protected from themselves. In order to spare those who wanted to come up to Mount Sinai, which was holy, God told Moses to "warn the people so they do not force their way through to see the LORD and many of them perish" (Exodus 19:21).

Some people are curious about the wrong things. Mass shooters often reveal a dark fascination with other shooters or serial killers. One of the most atrocious massacres that "inspired" subsequent carnage was the 1999 Columbine school shooting in Littleton, Colorado. Adam Lanza, who shot and killed twenty-six people, including twenty children between six and seven years old at Sandy Hook Elementary School in 2012, viewed the Columbine shooters as "ego-ideals."[12] High school senior Sol Pais was reportedly "infatuated" with the Columbine massacre and traveled to Colorado and purchased a shotgun shortly before the twentieth anniversary of the Columbine carnage.[13] Although she was later found dead from an apparent suicide, she had allegedly traveled to the Denver area as a "pilgrimage."[14]

Another unhealthy subject of interest that we are not supposed to dabble in is the occult, or the desire to know the future or communicate with the dead. The Bible clearly warns us not to seek out mediums (see Leviticus 19:31; Isaiah 8:19) and describes anyone who practices divination, sorcery, or witchcraft as "detestable" to God (Deuteronomy 18:10–12). Such predictions are also worthless: "All the counsel you have received has only worn you out! Let your astrologers come forward, those stargazers who make predictions month by month, let them save you from what is coming upon you" (Isaiah 47:13). An inquisitive spirit should be tempered with intelligence and godly insight.

> An inquisitive spirit should be tempered with intelligence and godly insight.

When Bad Looks Bold

"How do you know unless you try it?" Many of us endured that rite of passage question when we were young, and it is still asked today. You may remember the "double-dog dare" re-popularized in *A Christmas Story* with the frozen flagpole stunt. Unfortunately, daring behavior includes activities far more dangerous.

Boldness characterizes the righteous, not risk-takers. Nonetheless, normally cautious individuals are lured into perilous situations with taunting comments and modesty-shaming remarks, such as "You can't possibly be that old fashioned" or "Please tell me you are not going to be boring." But hesitancy signals hazard. There is a reason most people are reluctant to try a street drug at a party or drag race on the street. Despite the allure, many people obey their instincts and refrain from dangerous behavior. But not everyone. For some people, despite an appreciation of the risks, wrong looks right.

Also beware of people who encourage irresponsibility. In the words of Jesus, "If anyone causes one of these little ones—those who believe in me—to stumble, it would be better for them to have a large millstone hung around their neck and to be drowned in the depths of the sea" (Matthew 18:6).

Biblically, boldness comes from knowing Christ: "In him and through faith in him we may approach God with freedom and confidence" (Ephesians 3:12). Because we have confidence "through Christ before God" (2 Corinthians 3:4), we have hope and "are very bold" (2 Corinthians 3:12).

The Pleasure of Predictability

For a relaxing, rewarding lifestyle, choose safety over sensation-seeking, physical health over hedonism, and comfort over curiosity. After all, nothing is really ever "new." In other words,

"What has been will be again, what has been done will be done again; there is nothing new under the sun" (Ecclesiastes 1:9).

Variety is not always the spice of life. Whether presented as the temptation to try a dangerous new sport or stray from a committed relationship, chasing the latest fad can be destructive and dangerous. Especially since what is marketed as novel is frequently simply recycled and repackaged—often literally.

As opposed to seeking stimulation through a perilous lifestyle, find security in safety because God never changes (see Hebrews 13:8). "Every good and perfect gift is from above, coming down from the Father of the heavenly lights, who does not change like shifting shadows" (James 1:17). The comfort of certainty allows us to enjoy the pleasure of predictability and peace.

CHAPTER 13

WHEN DARKNESS LOOKS DESIRABLE

Light has come into the world,
but people loved darkness instead of light
because their deeds were evil.

JOHN 3:19

My case detective and I walk into a nondescript, nameless building to investigate a crime. Inside is a thriving, crowded adult jacuzzi establishment existing in almost total darkness punctuated with a smattering of neon lights, no doubt to shroud the nature of the activity inside. Many patrons scatter with a flash of the badge, worried about being exposed in more ways than one. What kind of people are in there? Some of the same ones you pass in corporate hallways or expensive restaurants. But their presence in the underground establishment, ready to be busted, reveals more about their repute than their résumé.

Many less provocative, socially acceptable settings intentionally incorporate the cover of darkness and the desirability of the dimmer switch. As we grow older, we joke that we look better with less light, but we are also less likely to be recognized. Nothing is wrong with a romantic candlelight dinner unless the dimly lit venue is designed to conceal an adulterous affair.

Some people patronize dark places to cover their tracks and conceal their identities. Nightclubs and gambling establishments often capitalize on and indeed cater to this appetite for anonymity by operating with less light. Some people are surprised when they get a good look at the company they are keeping during last call at the bar, when the house lights come on a few minutes later. Under the starkness of sudden fluorescent light, much is revealed because darkness conceals many different characteristics.

Malevolent actors exploit darkness. Movie theatres are dark to keep our focus on the screen, which has allowed mass shooters to prey upon an unsuspecting crowd's completely diverted attention. Thefts occur in movie theatres for the same reason: darkness conceals crime. Darkness also conceals criminal activity online; the dark web was created to facilitate deviance and illegality by connecting like-minded lawbreakers in an arena where communication is hard to trace. In many cases, darkness is not desirable; it is dangerous.

Darkness Is Dangerous

The prophet Isaiah decried not only the fate of those who labeled evil as good and good as evil but also those "who put darkness for light and light for darkness" (Isaiah 5:20). Darkness was one of the biblical plagues God brought on Egypt, described ominously as "darkness that can be felt" (Exodus 10:21). Without sufficient light, people suffer physically and emotionally, as experienced through seasonal affective disorder, which therapists often treat with light therapy. Darkness can be dangerous when it conceals hidden hazards. This is why we use nightlights and keep flashlights near our beds in case of power outages.

Darkness is not desirable; it is dangerous.

The analogy of light versus dark can also describe human behavior: "The path of the righteous is like the morning sun, shining ever brighter till the full light of day. But the way of the wicked is like deep darkness; they do not know what makes them stumble" (Proverbs 4:18–19). We recognize character through the light of one's life. "If we claim to have fellowship with him and yet walk in the darkness, we lie and do not live out the truth" (1 John 1:6). It is important to perceive this type of hypocrisy sooner rather than later because Paul warns us not to be unequally yoked with unbelievers, as he asks, "What do righteousness and wickedness have in common? Or what fellowship can light have with darkness?" (2 Corinthians 6:14). Thankfully, we don't have to walk in darkness or be lured to the dark side by those who do because Christ is the Light of the World.

The Light of the World

Light comes from God, "and God said, 'Let there be light,' and there was light. God saw that the light was good, and he separated the light from the darkness" (Genesis 1:3–4). Jesus explains, "I am the light of the world. Whoever follows me will never walk in darkness, but will have the light of life" (John 8:12). He brings life as the light of humankind, light that shines in the darkness and cannot be overcome (see 1:4–5).

Moving from darkness to light implies a change in lifestyle. "For you were once darkness, but now you are light in the Lord. Live as children of light" (Ephesians 5:8). Jesus sent Paul to preach the gospel in order to turn his listeners "from darkness to light" (Acts 26:18). Paul referred to new believers as "children of the light and children of the day" who "do not belong to the night or to the darkness" (1 Thessalonians 5:5). As Paul wrote to the Corinthians, "For God, who said, 'Let light shine out of darkness,' made his light shine in our hearts to give us the light of the knowledge of God's glory displayed in the face of Christ" (2 Corinthians 4:6).

We are to avoid darkness: "Have nothing to do with the fruitless deeds of darkness, but rather expose them" (Ephesians 5:11). Just as my case detective and I exposed the criminal activity at the bath house, deeds done in darkness are eventually revealed. Contrary to the popular slogan "What happens in Vegas stays in Vegas," what people do in secret is almost always eventually revealed:

> There is nothing concealed that will not be disclosed, or hidden that will not be made known. What you have said in the dark will be heard in the daylight, and what you have whispered in the ear in the inner rooms will be proclaimed from the roofs. (Luke 12:2–3)

Because of God's mercy, "the rising sun will come to us from heaven to shine on those living in darkness and in the shadow of death, to guide our feet into the path of peace" (Luke 1:78–79).

CHAPTER 14

WHEN LUST FEELS LIKE LOVE

*The lust of the flesh, the lust of the eyes, and the pride of life—
comes not from the Father but from the world.*

1 JOHN 2:16

Sexual sin is specifically addressed in the Bible. Paul warned the Corinthians to "flee from sexual immorality. All other sins a person commits are outside the body, but whoever sins sexually, sins against their own body" (1 Corinthians 6:18). God's will for us is sanctification: to avoid sexual immorality and learn to control our own bodies "in a way that is holy and honorable, not in passionate lust like…[those] who do not know God" (1 Thessalonians 4:3–5). Because our bodies were "not meant for sexual immorality" (1 Corinthians 6:13) but are temples of the Holy Spirit, we are reminded to honor God with our bodies (vv. 19–20).

One of the most tragic examples of the destructive force of lust is found in the book of Judges: the story of Sampson and

Delilah. The Bible introduces us to Samson's penchant for stubbornly following his desire in chapter 15, when he married a woman against the advice of his parents, and it proved to be a union that, indeed, ended in disaster. His response to his parents was revealing when they originally questioned his judgment, "Get her for me, for she looks good to me" (Judges 14:3 NASB1995).

After the first marriage failed, Samson met and fell in love with Delilah. But unbeknownst to him, the Philistine rulers bribed Delilah: "See if you can lure him into showing you the secret of his great strength and how we can overpower him so we may tie him up and subdue him" (Judges 16:5). Sure enough, although he held out as long as he could, Delilah, perhaps because love blinds, persuaded Samson to reveal his weakness to her through continual questioning and "nagging" (vv. 16–17). Her ruse led to Samson's downfall, including having his captors literally blind him.

Why didn't Samson question Delilah's need to know his vulnerability and how he could be exploited? This is the type of question I often ask my financial crime victims, who willingly agreed to share their bank account information with others. Many explain that their judgment was compromised because they were enamored with the questioner, as Samson was, or wanted to avoid confrontation to preserve the relationship with the person trying to dupe them. With seemingly smooth sailing in a sea of pleasurable emotion, some feel a reluctance to make waves or rock the boat. Other biblical accounts similarly illustrate how lust masquerading as love can leave a trail of tragedy.

Second Samuel 13 recounts the story of how King David's son Amnon fell "in love" with his half-sister Tamar, who was a virgin. He deceitfully strategized a ruse to be alone with her, pretending to be ill, and forcibly raped her (see vv. 6–14). Immediately afterward, Amnon hated her with such intense hatred that "he hated her more than he had loved her" (v. 15). Amnon's brother Absalom killed him several years later, which had been his "express intention" ever since he found out about the rape (v. 32).

Genesis 34 recounts the rape of Dinah, one of the daughters of Jacob. Her assailant Shechem, after he had raped her, decided he loved and wanted to marry her (see vv. 2–4). But because their sister had been defiled, Jacob's sons tricked Shechem and his father and ended up killing both of them as well as all of the men of their city (see vv. 25–26).

Even King Solomon was led astray by lustful passion. He loved women, having "seven hundred wives…and three hundred concubines." Unfortunately, as smart as he was, his wives "led him astray" and "turned his heart after other gods" (1 Kings 11:3–4).

All the Wrong Places

We instinctively recognize that we meet different types of people in different settings. The ideal scenario for meeting "the one" is usually not in the middle of the night in a smoky dive bar with dollar drinks and a dartboard. But sometimes, regardless of where you meet someone, the emotional experience is the same. Lust feels like love.

Samson defied his parent's warnings regarding where he should meet a prospective wife, instead becoming engaged to a woman he saw and immediately described as the "right one" (Judges 14:3). As we know, she betrayed his confidence, leading to Samson striking down a number of Philistines while his "wife was given to one of his companions" (vv. 19–20).

Sometimes we intentionally mingle with the wrong crowd. Attending a concert or event on the "wrong side" of town or off the beaten path might seem exciting. But depending on whom you meet there, walking down a path with an unapologetic, rebellious wolf in wolf's clothing may be walking the gangplank. When people lead you astray by showcasing and glamourizing their dangerous qualities, what you see is what you get. In addition, the type of people you meet in the "wrong places" may be emotionally or physically abusive, sexually aggressive, disrespectful, or unkind. Lustful liaisons can breed toxic relationships characterized by unhealthy demands and expectations.

Despite the potential for initial intrigue, over the long-term, with both love and friendship, opposites do not continue to attract. Successful couples often have different but complementary qualities and are accordingly better together.

The Wrong Kind of Love

When lust feels like love, the resulting sexual behavior might be physically satisfying in the short term but emotionally and relationally damaging over time. This is true even within committed relationships. One example of how "loving" couples damage their relationship is through the consumption of pornography.

Normalized and rationalized by many, pornography is a poor substitute for authentic affection. Graphic sexual content involves the exploitation of (often young) men and women, is harmful and addictive, and has a detrimental impact on romantic relationships. A rich body of research documents the harmful effects of pornography on individuals and relationships. Beyond evidence that the use of pornography decreases a relationship's quality, research reveals a positive link between problematic use of pornography and both physical and sexual intimate partner abuse.[15] And for both men and women, a higher amount of pornography use is linked with having a lower likelihood of intervening to prevent an act of sexual assault.[16]

Viewing graphic sexual material can also create false expectations and sexual insecurity. Researchers found that, for women, prior exposure to pornography was linked with higher insecurities about physical appearance as well as decreased enjoyment of physical expressions of intimacy.[17]

Further research links prolonged use of pornography to sexual offending, incorporating a desire to act out the deviant sexual acts depicted, especially when viewing violent pornography.[18] Watching graphic sexual content desensitizes viewers, adversely impacts attitudes toward women and sexuality, perpetuates rape myths, promotes sexual harassment, and increases the risk of engaging in physically assaultive behavior.

In addition, perhaps not surprisingly, pornography use has been linked to loneliness.[19] Viewing such content disrupts bonding with a partner, leading to relational detachment and dissatisfaction. Pornography's sexual script, promoting the objectification of women along with the affirmation of misogyny and promiscuity, negates the type of relational attachment that increases intimacy.

Smart relational partners exercise better judgment: "I will not look with approval on anything that is vile" (Psalm 101:3). The Bible prioritizes life over lust: "Turn my eyes away from worthless things; preserve my life according to your word" (119:37). We are encouraged to reject things that belong to our "earthly nature," which include lust, sexual immorality, and impurity (see Colossians 3:5), and instead to walk by the Spirit, to avoid gratifying the desires of the flesh (see Galatians 5:16). "Let us purify ourselves from everything that contaminates body and spirit, perfecting holiness out of reverence for God" (2 Corinthians 7:1).

Recognizing True Love

Love does not appear at first sight; it develops over time as a couple builds a relationship of trust and respect. Many people who have been swept off their feet in a whirlwind romance that took off too quickly can tell you that such relationships often crash and burn. Tragically, social norms promote relational scripts that perpetuate such defeat. From reality television to the public displays of affection by red carpet celebrity couples, Hollywood portrayals of unrealistic expectations lead to delusion, disillusion, and disappointment.

Love does not appear at first sight; it develops over time.

True love is not only patient and kind, but it is also without envy or pride. Love does not dishonor others, is selfless, and is slow to anger. And true love "keeps no record of wrongs" (1 Corinthians 13:4–5). When was the last time you were in a relationship with a partner like this? If you can think of someone who fits the bill, chances are you are still together because he or she is a keeper.

CHAPTER 15

WHEN IMMORAL SEEMS NORMAL

Marriage should be honored by all,
and the marriage bed kept pure,
for God will judge the adulterer and all the sexually immoral.

HEBREWS 13:4

A glib salesperson might joke with a man buying lingerie, asking whether he is buying for his wife, girlfriend, or mistress. When did infidelity become funny? Unsurprisingly, infidelity is no laughing matter to anyone suffering from such betrayal. While adultery might not always be predictable, it is preventable by avoiding forbidden fruit.

If a married man wants to have lunch with an attractive ex-girlfriend, his wife might think she has nothing to worry about if she trusts her husband. But biblical wisdom would identify the issue as not about trust but temptation. Old flames should be off limits. What is the purpose of the lunch date? What if the rendezvous rekindles a spark? Unfortunately, sometimes that is precisely the goal.

But whether or not a spouse intends to be unfaithful, why head down that path? For many people, there is no such thing as "just looking." As Jesus explains, anyone who looks at a woman with lustful intent "has already committed adultery with her in his heart" (Matthew 5:28). Fanning old flames can also create an appearance of impropriety. Consider how a "lunch date" with an ex-paramour might look from the perspective of mutual friends or colleagues, particularly those who are predisposed to gossip. Before long, a rumor catches fire. Why create the spark? Enjoy lunch and lively conversation with friends or family instead.

Resisting Taboo

When asked to think about forbidden love, many people default to *Romeo and Juliet* or Tony and Maria in *West Side Story*. People who work in agencies with fraternization rules think about covert coworker couplings, and as a prosecutor, I worry about child predators. Although examples of off-limits relationships abound, one of the most damaging types of inappropriate pairings involves infidelity.

Infidelity was as problematic in Old Testament times as it is today. "You shall not commit adultery" is one of the Ten Commandments (Exodus 20:14), and the Lord tells the prophet that rebellious people are "well-fed, lusty stallions, each neighing for another man's wife" (Jeremiah 5:8). Adultery destroys marriages, ruins relationships, betrays friends, devastates trust, and damages people personally. "A man who commits adultery has no sense; whoever does so destroys himself" (Proverbs 6:32).

Scripture provides guidance to resist the temptation. For instance, Proverbs 6:24 counsels a man to keep away from his neighbor's wife and from "the smooth talk of a wayward woman." He is warned, "Do not lust in your heart after her beauty or let her captivate you with her eyes" (v. 25) and asked, "Can a man scoop fire into his lap without his clothes being burned? Can a man walk on hot coals without his feet being scorched?" (vv. 27–28). In other words, avoid forbidden fruit.

The consequences of adultery are both spiritual and practical, often setting into motion a tragic series of events that cannot be undone. King David learned this lesson the hard way. Having stayed behind during a time when kings went off to war, he was walking on the roof of his palace when he spotted a woman bathing who was "very beautiful" (2 Samuel 11:2). Just as someone today might ask an acquaintance about an attractive stranger, David sent someone to inquire about the identity of the woman he saw from the roof. But even after he discovered the woman was Bathsheba, "wife of Uriah," David was driven by desire. He ordered messengers to have her brought to him, slept with her, and had her husband killed (see vv. 3–16).

David's actions displeased God (v. 27). Although he subsequently confessed, repented, and received forgiveness, David not only lost the first son he and Bathsheba conceived, but the sword also never departed from his house because of his sin (see chapter 12). Sin always has consequences.

Resisting sexual sin, on the other hand, is rewarded in the end. Genesis 37 relates the story of Joseph, who refused to engage in adultery with Potiphar, his master's wife. After his brothers sold him into slavery, Joseph was purchased by Potiphar, "one of Pharaoh's officials, the captain of the guard" (v. 36). Joseph was a man of God, but because he was also "well-built and handsome," he captured the attention of his master's wife, who continually implored him to sleep with her, even though he continued to refuse (see 39:6–10). Although she eventually made a false allegation of attempted rape that initially landed him in prison, Joseph eventually became a national leader when Pharoah, recognizing him as "one in whom is the spirit of God," put him in charge of all of Egypt (see 41:38–41).

Resisting temptation often requires avoiding it in the first place. This involves discipline. "I made a covenant with my eyes not to look lustfully at a young woman" (Job 31:1). Worldly temptation does not come from God; each of us is tempted when we are overcome by our "own evil desire and enticed" (James 1:14). But God can help us resist. "No temptation has overtaken you except what is common to mankind. And God is faithful; he will not let you be tempted beyond what you can bear. But when you are tempted, he will also provide a way out so that you can endure it" (1 Corinthians 10:13).

> Resisting temptation often requires avoiding it
> in the first place.

The Covenant of Marriage

Drive-through wedding chapels in Las Vegas illustrate the light-hearted view of a serious commitment. Marriage is an analogy of Christ's relationship with the church. As lawyers, we handle contracts, which are often broken and sometimes not even enforceable, whereas marriage is a covenant, designed to be a lifelong union till death do we part.

The high divorce rate we experience in modern society was never God's plan for marriage. To the contrary, the plan was that "a man leaves his father and mother and is united to his wife, and they become one flesh" (Genesis 2:24). When the Pharisees asked Jesus about divorce, he explained that:

> At the beginning the Creator "made them male and female," and said, "For this reason a man will leave his father and mother and be united to his wife, and the two will become one flesh"…What God has joined together, let no one separate." (Matthew 19:4–6)

Marriage was also a way to prevent the immoral from becoming normal. Matrimony prevents immorality by providing a solution to the temptation to engage in sexual sin: "Each man should have sexual relations with his own wife, and each woman with her own husband" (1 Corinthians 7:2). Marriage was also designed to afford newlyweds time to celebrate their union. In the Old Testament, a newly married man was not to be sent to war or otherwise burdened for one year, during which time he was free to stay home "and bring happiness to the wife he has married" (Deuteronomy 24:5). What a concept! We all know couples who were both so busy they skipped a honeymoon, never mind taking an extended amount of time to themselves to celebrate the marriage.

Relationships grow and flourish when they are planted in healthy soil and nurtured with the right ingredients, not when they are tried and tempted through dangerous liaisons. Invest in a healthy, happy relationship that will stand the test of time.

CHAPTER 16

WHEN FRENEMIES LOOK LIKE FRIENDS

The righteous choose their friends carefully,
but the way of the wicked leads them astray.
PROVERBS 12:26

We all have a basic human need to belong, but companionship is a choice. Or as Amos 3:3 echoes by posing the following question: "Do two walk together unless they have agreed to do so?" In order to fulfill our need for friends or companions, people join a variety of groups and clubs. Some choose to join cults and gangs. In both, the sense of belonging might feel the same, but joiner beware: within some types of groups, foes masquerade as friends. That's why we must carefully choose the company we keep, including the friends we choose to trust.

Being part of a clique is a critically important part of adolescence for many young people, to the extent that social exclusion can be emotionally devastating. From teasing to bullying or worse, young people suffer emotionally when they don't feel accepted. But if our precious young men and women choose the wrong friends merely to be part of a group, they may be led astray, adversely influenced, and even end up guilty by association. Solomon warns us, "Do not make friends with a hot-tempered person, do not associate with one easily angered, or you may learn their ways and get yourself ensnared" (Proverbs 22:24–25). Yet if the hot-tempered, anger-prone individual is famous or popular, he or she may be an enticing associate.

Beware the allure of the in-crowd. In distinguishing friends from frenemies, forget about attraction, wealth, or popularity. People who are untrustworthy and unpredictable do not make good friends, and they are not a good influence, and the wisdom of Proverbs tells us that "one who has unreliable friends soon comes to ruin" (18:24).

The Company You Keep

Growing up, I often heard adults remark, "Show me your friends, and I'll show you your future." Do we still warn our children like this? We should. Whoever spends their time with the wise becomes wise, but anyone who prefers the company of fools will suffer harm (see 13:20). Proverbs further warns us to avoid fools who lack knowledge (see 14:7).

When King Solomon's son Rehoboam took the throne, his subjects implored him to lighten their workload. He consulted with his elders, who advised him to answer the people favorably in order to retain their loyalty. But he decided to follow the bad advice of the young men he grew up with instead, who encouraged him to answer harshly, which led to rebellion (see 1 Kings 12:1–16).

Bad company is a corrupting influence (see 1 Corinthians 15:33). "Like a muddied spring or a polluted well are the righteous who give way to the wicked" (Proverbs 25:26). We also know that "friendship with the world means enmity against God" (James 4:4). When we choose not to join others in a lifestyle of lust, debauchery, overindulgence, and idolatry, the group or person is surprised that we choose not to participate in their "reckless, wild living" and might even abuse us for our restraint (1 Peter 4:3–4).

So how do we choose our friends wisely? Remember that actions speak louder than words. Paul says to avoid anyone "who claims to be a brother or sister" but is greedy, sexually immoral, slanderous, or prone to idolatry, theft, or drunkenness. He even advises us to avoid eating with such people (1 Corinthians 5:11).

In advising believers not to "be yoked together with unbelievers," Paul points to the striking lack of common ground between the two worldviews. "For what do righteousness and wickedness have in common? Or what fellowship can light have with darkness?" (2 Corinthians 6:14). Yet many people never uncover this level of detail in others; they are seduced by superficial similarity. Look deeper.

Red Flags of False Friends

The Bible explicitly details what people will be like in the last days: "People will be lovers of themselves, lovers of money, boastful, proud, abusive, disobedient to their parents, ungrateful, unholy, without love, unforgiving, slanderous, without self-control, brutal, not lovers of the good, treacherous, rash, conceited, lovers of pleasure rather than lovers of God" (2 Timothy 3:1–4). As you might expect after reading that list of traits, Paul tells us to avoid these people (v. 5). Good advice—assuming we *recognize* them. Unfortunately, we often don't because some people are quite good at hiding their venom behind a veneer.

Consider the friend who inappropriately and publicly reveals intimate information you shared with her privately, whether stemming from poor manners or malice. However, you exercised poor judgment in your selection of a confidant. One way to choose friends carefully is to listen to the way they talk about other people. It gives you a sneak preview of how they will likely talk about you.

One way to choose friends carefully is to listen to the way they talk about other people. It gives you a sneak preview of how they will likely talk about you.

Many workplaces contain people with mean spirits. This callous jokester is often surrounded by a crowd of laughing coworkers at the water cooler. From a distance, you would not peg this comedic, outwardly fun-loving employee as dangerous. But once you get close enough to hear that his selection of humor is at the expense of others, you should.

Scripture advises us to be wary of people who are prone to speaking out of turn because "a gossip betrays a confidence; so avoid anyone who talks too much" (Proverbs 20:19). Malevolent malcontents who are quick to find fault in others are not wise choices for friends. "Grumblers and faultfinders" are included within the description of ungodly "scoffers" who follow evil desires as they "boast about themselves and flatter others for their own advantage" (Jude 1:16–18). These people divide others as they "follow mere natural instincts and do not have the Spirit" (v. 19). Creating conflict within a community is detestable to the Lord (see Proverbs 6:16–19).

Some child predators have false friends. A few of the schoolteachers I have prosecuted for having sex with their students have had best friends who were teenagers, illustrating deviant peer group identification. This can be confusing to the teenager who sees the adult teacher as a role model and mentor, unaware of the psychology behind the predatory behavior.

True Friendship

The biblical version of friendship is starkly different from the type of friendships glorified in the world. True friends are not fickle or fair-weather. "A friend loves at all times, and a brother is born for a time of adversity" (Proverbs 17:17). In fact, a true friend seeks to reconcile your relationship not when they are upset with you but when they know you have something against them (see Matthew 5:23–24). True friends can also serve as accountability partners, making sure both of you stay on the right path.

Like the court support dog that some of my child witnesses are allowed to have under the witness stand to pet as they testify, true friends are a calming influence. They make you feel valued regardless of your attributes because, for godly friends, favoritism is forbidden (see James 2:1–4).

Friends Forgive

True friends do not hold grudges. They forgive and do so repeatedly. Peter asked Jesus how many times he should forgive a brother or sister who had sinned against him: "Up to seven times?" Jesus replied, "Not seven times, but seventy-seven times" (Matthew 18:21–22). Instead of grievance collecting, we are instructed to "bear with each other and forgive one another if any of you has a grievance against someone. Forgive as the Lord forgave you" (Colossians 3:13). Extending forgiveness clears a path for our prayers as well, as Jesus instructed us, "When you stand praying, if you hold anything against anyone, forgive them, so that your Father in heaven may forgive you your sins" (Mark 11:25).

When we forgive each other, we acknowledge our own vulnerability. "Brothers and sisters, if someone is caught in a sin, you who live by the Spirit should restore that person gently. But watch yourselves, or you also may be tempted" (Galatians 6:1). Paul explained how we are to forgive offenders who are truly repentant, instructing the Corinthians to follow punishment with emotional reinstatement: "You ought to forgive and comfort him, so that he will not be overwhelmed by excessive sorrow. I urge you, therefore, to reaffirm your love for him" (2 Corinthians 2:7–8).

Ultimately, the way a person treats their friends speaks volumes about their faith. When we love God, we must love our brothers and sisters (see 1 John 4:20–21). And a good friend stays closer than a brother (see Proverbs 18:24).

CHAPTER 17

THE OPTICS OF OCCUPATION

May the favor of the Lord our God rest on us;
establish the work of our hands.

Psalm 90:17

When picking juries, one of the first questions we ask the potential jurors is what they do for a living. Why? Because we can infer much about what someone is like by knowing how they spend their time. Or can we? We assume that nurses and nannies are naturally caring and kind with hearts of gold. We adorn all types of caregivers or anyone who helps the less fortunate with a cloak of respectability. Yet even within helping professions, not everyone is as genuine and trustworthy as their titles and positions may suggest. Some of the most heinous offenses I have prosecuted have involved the exploitation of the vulnerable by their caregivers, who betray positions of trust. Job titles reveal professional qualifications, not quality character.

The Pretext of Titles

When an individual is introduced as "Lord Conroy," "Lady Claire," or "her Royal Highness," we sit up and take notice. And chances are that we are likely already in a state of attention if we are at an event mingling with royalty. Titles convey status, rank, authority, and many other things. Most people have a variety of credentialed acquaintances addressed as everything from "doctor" in the emergency room to "your honor" in the courtroom to "congresswoman" in the Capitol to "Father" in the pulpit. Yet before we become overly impressed, we cannot automatically assume someone with an important title leads a good life.

> Not everyone is as genuine and trustworthy as their titles and positions may suggest.

True, many talented, smart people with lofty titles are indeed compassionate, kind, and trustworthy. But not always. And sometimes credentials are counterfeit, such as when people creatively embellish alter egos. Some titles exist solely for the purpose of designing a business card. When you meet an "account professional" or a "senior manager," you probably want to know what they actually do. What kind of accounts? Senior manager of what? You would want to know the same thing about someone who says they're "in sales." Do they sell draperies or drugs? And for someone who identifies broadly as a preacher or teacher, dogma and doctrine can be descriptive and defining.

There are some occupations we do not traditionally view positively. The Pharisees asked Jesus why he ate with "tax collectors and sinners" after he had just selected a tax collector as one of his disciples and was dining at his house (see Mark 2:14–16). Yet there is an emphasis on separating the person from the profession. When tax collectors came to John the Baptist and asked what they should do, John's advice was straightforward: "Don't collect any more than you are required to" (Luke 3:12–13). Paul emphasized the requirement to submit to authority out of not only fear of punishment but also conscience, explaining, "This is also why you pay taxes, for the authorities are God's servants, who give their full time to governing" (Romans 13:5–6).

You can also learn something about a person by the type of work that they choose, assuming they had a choice and were not forced to take whatever they could get to make ends meet. But you can discern much more by observing how they approach their employment. You wouldn't expect to get a text message from an air traffic controller during her shift or see a law enforcement professional flash a badge off duty in hopes of obtaining an undeserved benefit. Income doesn't equate with integrity, but choice of profession often reflects personality.

The Value of Work Ethic

The world's first man, Adam, had a job to do: "The Lord God took the man and put him in the Garden of Eden to work it and take care of it" (Genesis 2:15). Jesus worked as a carpenter (see Mark 6:3). Working is beneficial to the worker. "Those who work their land will have abundant food" (Proverbs 12:11). There is value in self-sufficiency as the Bible encourages us to "mind your own business and work with your hands…so that your daily life may win the respect of outsiders and so that you will not be dependent on anybody" (1 Thessalonians 4:11–12). Hard work yields profit, while "mere talk leads only to poverty" (Proverbs 14:23). "The craving of a sluggard will be the death of him, because his hands refuse to work" (21:25).

Paul models an admirable work ethic while sharing the gospel with the early church: "Surely you remember, brothers and sisters, our toil and hardship; we worked night and day in order not to be a burden to anyone while we preached the gospel of God to you" (1 Thessalonians 2:9). There was no freeloading.

But regardless of title, we should also examine the nature of someone's work today as opposed to when they began the job, sometimes decades ago. When an employee has spent an entire career at one company, he or she may be favorably misjudged as a worker of great integrity. "You can trust him; he's been here forever." If I had a dime for every time I heard that from an employer who discovered that a longtime employee was stealing from the company, I would be able to retire.

Criminally minded employees know that longevity facilitates familiarity, as well as access to resources. We can call this having credentials of consistency. And illegality aside, as a practical matter, not every company veteran is valuable. The most prestigious workplaces have dead weight in the form of employees who once were passionate about their careers but are now pushing paper, still earning six-figure incomes. This is unhelpful to the company and unhelpful to other employees: "One who is slack in his work is brother to one who destroys" (Proverbs 18:9).

On the other hand, many young blue-collar workers arrive at work each day ready to tackle their jobs with energy and enthusiasm. What they lack in experience, they make up for in effort, modeling the wisdom of King Solomon: "Whatever your hand finds to do, do it with all your might" (Ecclesiastes 9:10).

Paul also reminds us well that we are not only working for human employers: "Whatever you do, work at it with all your heart, as working for the Lord, not for human masters" (Colossians 3:23). Accordingly, we often learn the most about someone through the way they approach the job that they do. Whether selling insurance, saving lives, or serving food, "Do your best to present yourself to God as one approved, a worker who does not need to be ashamed and who correctly handles the word of truth" (2 Timothy 2:15).

The Labor of Love

Some people believe they can work themselves into positions of prestige and power, not recognizing the futility of working for its own sake. To the contrary, we are reminded, "it is by grace you have been saved, through faith—and this is not from yourselves, it is the gift of God— not by works, so that no one can boast" (Ephesians 2:8–9).

We bless others when, instead of laboring only for ourselves, we allow Christ to work through us. Through the Holy Spirit, we are designed to be team players who work together in community:

> Christ himself gave the apostles, the prophets, the evangelists, the pastors and teachers, to equip his people for works of service, so that the body of Christ may be built up until we all reach unity in the faith and in the knowledge of the Son of God and become mature, attaining to the whole measure of the fullness of Christ. (Ephesians 4:11–13)

We are meant to use our spiritual gifts to benefit the greater good. As Paul explained to the Corinthians, "each of you has your own gift from God; one has this gift, another has that" (1 Corinthians 7:7). In the words of the apostle Peter, "Each of you should use whatever gift you have received to serve others, as faithful stewards of God's grace in its various forms. If anyone speaks, they should do so as one who speaks the very words of God. If anyone serves, they should do so with the strength God provides" (1 Peter 4:10–11).

When we use our gifts and talents to bless the people around us, we are working in a fashion that demonstrates our love for others as the world around us demonstrates God's love for us. "The heavens declare the glory of God; the skies proclaim the work of his hands" (Psalm 19:1). "For you make me glad by your deeds, LORD; I sing for joy at what your hands have done" (92:4). We pray that God may bless others through our work as well.

CHAPTER 18

WHEN CREDENTIALS DO NOT REVEAL CHARACTER

*In everything set them an example
by doing what is good.*
TITUS 2:7

One of the most memorable serial child molesters I prosecuted was a well-credentialed man I had met at a Rotary Club meeting and with whom I had, apparently, been impressed—as a colleague remembered who didn't reveal the connection until I had completed the case. The high-profile defendant, a well-regarded philanthropist who even had a day named after him in my city, was masterful at concealing the fetish behind the façade.

Have you ever been so impressed with a description of someone's past that you can't wait to meet them in the present? Enamored with their list of accomplishments and feats, you have already crowned them with glory and honor. You have assumed everything you've heard about them is true and was done in pursuit of benevolence. Both of those assumptions are risky and rushed. A list of accomplishments may be the brightest side of someone's history, while their dark side might be the rest of the story, which I have the job of proving in court.

The Pretense of Prestige

I have met many impressive community figures throughout the course of my career whose excellent reputation preceded them—and protected them. One of the most difficult types of cases to prosecute is one involving a defendant with clout. Politicians, public figures, and esteemed community members are challenging suspects given their air of authority, based on their position of public trust. Initially, a popular public official looks the same standing behind a podium giving a keynote speech in a ballroom as he does sitting in the defendant's chair in a courtroom. But then the case begins.

Nothing is quite like the first day of presenting a multi-count sex crime case against a defendant in a courtroom literally packed to capacity with his or her supporters. Against a backdrop of passionate community members expressing their loyalty with buttons and T-shirts, the accused looks like a hero. But as the trial proceeds, the tide begins to turn. Being outnumbered does not mean being outmatched because I have the advantage of evidence. You see, most of those supporters are not there because they know the defendant personally; they know him or her only through reputation. Accordingly and inevitably, as witness after witness shows up to testify, the crowd thins—as does the defendant's cloak of credibility. The beloved protagonist begins to look like a predator.

We can't judge character through community credentials or a curriculum vitae because degrees can deceive. Again, the Unabomber, Ted Kaczynski, who mailed or delivered sixteen package bombs, killing three people and injuring twenty-three, graduated from Harvard and had a PhD in mathematics from the University of Michigan before teaching at Berkeley.[20] James Holmes, who killed twelve people and injured seventy others at a midnight showing of *The Dark Knight Rises* in Aurora, Colorado, was a PhD student in the "elite" neuroscience graduate program at the University of Colorado.[21]

Credentials can actually create suspicion when someone doesn't use them. As an educator, I am aware that some professional students collect degrees. But in most cases, people pursue an education within an area of both interest and expertise. A well-educated freeloader might simply be having fun or might be a fugitive. Someone on the run from the law who can pass rigorous board exams but not a background check may befriend a gullible benefactor with a big heart and deep pockets.

Qualifications Do Not Ensure Quality

An increasing number of jobs do, in fact, require background checks. But the absence of a criminal record does not ensure the presence of character. But other job requirements might. For example, certain character traits are required for important positions within the church. A church leader must be "above reproach, faithful to his wife, temperate, self-controlled, respectable, hospitable, able to teach" (1 Timothy 3:2). When was the last time you saw those requirements on a secular job description? You certainly won't find them listed on a résumé, although they are perhaps the most important requirements of any job, certainly a position of trust.

Note that the church leader's requirement is not merely to *have* a wife. Some of the sexual predators I have prosecuted admitted entering into sham marriages in order to avoid suspicion of pedophilia. The focus is on moral standards, not marital status.

But on the other hand, we should not automatically trust all religious leaders. In judging quality character from qualifications, the apostle John advises us not to believe everything we hear but to "test the spirits to see whether they are from God, because many false prophets have gone out into the world" (1 John 4:1). Jesus warned his disciples, "Watch out that no one deceives you. For many will come in my name, claiming, 'I am the Messiah,' and will deceive many" (Matthew 24:4–5).

Character through Christ

In reality, godly qualifications come not through the world but from the Word: "All Scripture is God-breathed and is useful for teaching, rebuking, correcting and training in righteousness, so that the servant of God may be thoroughly equipped for every good work" (2 Timothy 3:16–17). And we are promised that "he who began a good work in you will carry it on to completion until the day of Christ Jesus" (Philippians 1:6).

> Godly qualifications come not through the world
> but from the Word.

And because many jobs require both a résumé and referrals, righteous people can serve as living letters of recommendation. Paul writes to the Corinthians, "Do we need, like some people, letters of recommendation to you or from you? You yourselves are our letter, written on our hearts, known and read by everyone" (2 Corinthians 3:1–2). Quality comes from intentionality. "In your teaching show integrity, seriousness and soundness of speech that cannot be condemned, so that those who oppose you may be ashamed because they have nothing bad to say about us" (Titus 2:7–8). "And whatever you do, whether in word or deed, do it all in the name of the Lord Jesus, giving thanks to God the Father through him" (Colossians 3:17).

CHAPTER 19

THE RUSE OF REPUTATION

A good name is better than fine perfume.
ECCLESIASTES 7:1

If you heard that your favorite movie star was coming to your city for a public event, would you try to go see them? For many people who would, their interest stems from the fact that, although they do not personally know celebrities and other famous people, the reputation of those people precedes them. But the important question is: Reputation for what?

Nothing is wrong with being curious about other people. And as evidenced by the crowds, people who turn out to see rock stars, rulers, and royalty are in good company. But whether motivated by admiration or curiosity, in most cases, star-spotting involves observing a persona, not a person. To simply celebrate celebrity is to be blinded by the limelight. You may recognize names or pretty faces featured in the society pages of magazines or prancing down the red carpet at Hollywood awards shows without knowledge of their particular claim to fame. Newsflash: sometimes there isn't one. From A-list socialites to internet influencers, some people are simply famous for being famous.

In order to exercise good judgment, before you get excited about someone, consider what he or she is famous *for*. Some movie stars are famous for their award-winning ability to portray challenging characters; others become famous for being controversial characters in their private lives, to the extent a celebrity can have one anyway.

True, some Hollywood stars shine brightly as role models, mentors, and compassionate philanthropists, donating millions of dollars to charitable causes. But not everyone. As high-profile scandals involving famous people continually demonstrate, celebrity is unrelated to integrity, and sometimes fame is infamy. For some notorious characters, famous for all of the wrong reasons, there is no such thing as bad press. People recognize their name, not their deeds. We are reminded that the opposite should be true. "The name of the righteous is used in blessings, but the name of the wicked will rot" (Proverbs 10:7).

As some of my economic crime victims found out the hard way, some people with a reputation for having power and wealth actually have neither. Anyone who is lured into a relationship through false pretenses ends up in a life of empty promises and unfulfilled expectations. Status can be a smoke screen, clouding a clear view of the person behind the persona. "One person pretends to be rich, yet has nothing; another pretends to be poor, yet has great wealth" (13:7). King Solomon gives some good advice here, noting it is "better to be a nobody and yet have a servant than pretend to be somebody and have no food" (12:9).

Treasuring Talent

Many people have been blessed with genuine talent but do not use their talent wisely. Aptitudes like speaking, writing, or playing music can be used in many different ways. But I have prosecuted plenty of people who were talented at picking locks and hacking computers, ironically smart and resourceful enough to have landed high-paying, legitimate jobs. But because talented criminals often escape detection, how do we evaluate the merit of talent? Often through examining how someone *uses* the abilities they have.

In the early days of Christianity, the people of Samaria were impressed with Simon the sorcerer, who professed to be someone great and "amazed all the people," who declared that he was "rightly called the Great Power of God" (Acts 8:9–10). But when Philip came, proclaiming the true kingdom of God and Jesus Christ, he baptized new believers, including Simon, who "followed Philip everywhere, astonished by the great signs and miracles he saw" (v. 13). Peter and John brutally exposed Simon's false front when they came to the region imparting the Holy Spirit by the laying on of their hands, a God-given ability that Simon tried to buy from them so he could do it too (see vv. 14–24).

Jesus warns that false messiahs and prophets will perform impressive signs and wonders with the specific intention of deceiving others (see Matthew 24:23–24). Accordingly, remember to evaluate the integrity of someone based on more than just their apparent talent.

Judging Reputation from Location

When you meet someone new, you often ask where they are from. Even if someone is being specific (it is easy enough to be "from" the closest big city), geography does not predict credibility. True, you might be more inclined to trust someone if they are from a small mining town where everyone knows each other than if they are from Manhattan. But there are outliers within every community who are often overlooked because they are never seen in the first place.

After Jesus called Philip to follow him, Philip found Nathanael, explaining, "We have found the one Moses wrote about in the Law, and about whom the prophets also wrote—Jesus of Nazareth, the son of Joseph" (John 1:45). Nathanael responded by stereotyping: "Nazareth! Can anything good come from there?" To which Philip wisely responded, "Come and see" (v. 46). Seeing is believing because history can be deceiving—for better or for worse.

Seeing is believing because history can be deceiving—
for better or for worse.

Many people make the same mistake Nathanael did, judging personality and character from city or zip code. That is why some people have mailboxes in Beverly Hills, seeking prestige through postage. Yet many honest, hardworking individuals come from depressed or low-income areas while some manipulative white-collar thieves languish in luxury in high-end neighborhoods.

In misjudging a stranger as safe, another mistake is falling for the comfort of historical common ground. "She is from your hometown" someone might assure a skeptical mother who's choosing a nanny for her children, as if shared history indicates honesty. On the other hand, sometimes familiarity breeds contempt. "A prophet is not without honor except in his own town, among his relatives and in his own home" (Mark 6:4). Either way, a shared past impacts present perception.

The Standing of Godly Status

For some people, their reputation is admirable and accurate. King Solomon was the wisest man alive because his wisdom came directly from God. "God gave Solomon wisdom and very great insight, and a breadth of understanding as measureless as the sand on the seashore" (1 Kings 4:29). His reputation preceded him as "his fame spread to all the surrounding nations" (v. 31), and people came to listen from all over the world (v. 34).

The prophet Daniel had a worthy reputation that preceded him as well. After the terrifying episode in Daniel 5 where the king witnessed the disembodied handwriting on the wall, King Belshazzar of Babylon summoned Daniel in order to interpret the writing. As the king explained, "I have heard that the spirit of the gods is in you and that you have insight, intelligence and outstanding wisdom" (v. 14).

Joseph, who had the God-given ability to interpret dreams, was summoned by Pharaoh, the king of Egypt, who said, "I have heard it said of you that when you hear a dream you can interpret it" (Genesis 41:15). Joseph explained that he could not do it, but God could, and proceeded to interpret Pharaoh's dream, prompting Pharaoh to remove Joseph from the "dungeon" where he had been confined, place his own signet ring on Joseph's finger, and put Joseph in charge of all of Egypt (vv. 16–41). With reliable foreknowledge, reputation both precedes and accurately predicts.

CHAPTER 20

THE ILLUSION OF INTELLIGENCE

*God chose the foolish things of the world
to shame the wise.*
1 CORINTHIANS 1:27

You might have heard some common criminal law humor: "We never catch the smart ones." Actually we do, but we have a hard time convincing a judge and jury that they're guilty. Smart people often receive the benefit of the doubt. Articulate and accomplished, they appear composed and convincing.

But not all smart people are good people. We describe some people as too smart for their own good, those who look down on others or are intolerant and condescending. The Bible recognizes different types of intelligence as well. It contains the righteous wisdom of Solomon in the book of Proverbs but also chronicles the lives and deeds of nefarious characters who used their intellect to manipulate, exploit, and deceive. So before you are impressed with intelligence, consider the source of understanding.

Distinguishing Intelligence from Wisdom

The original apostles were students, not scholars. True, some were doctors and lawyers, but they were teachable. Others were persuasively impressive because of their lack of credentials. As recorded in Acts 4:13: "When they saw the courage of Peter and John and realized that they were unschooled, ordinary men, they were astonished and they took note that these men had been with Jesus." With the early apostles, their wisdom was apparent through their relationships, not their résumés.

True wisdom does not come from Harvard but from heaven. "The fear of the LORD is the beginning of wisdom, and knowledge of the Holy One is understanding" (Proverbs 9:10). Although Paul was well-educated and "thoroughly trained in the law" (Acts 22:3), he proclaimed to those he taught, "I did not come with eloquence or human wisdom as I proclaimed to you the testimony about God. For I resolved to know nothing while I was with you except Jesus Christ and him crucified" (1 Corinthians 2:1–2).

True wisdom does not come from Harvard but from heaven.

We are advised not to be wise in our own eyes (see Proverbs 3:7). The blessing of perceived intelligence can be a curse when it artificially inflates a sense of self-confidence. "The way of fools seems right to them, but the wise listen to advice" (12:15). Accordingly, we learn much about someone by how they respond to correction or criticism. "Do not rebuke mockers or they will hate you; rebuke the wise and they will love you. Instruct the wise and they will be wiser still; teach the righteous and they will add to their learning" (9:8–9).

True wisdom produces patience and the ability to overlook an offense (see 19:11). "Fools show their annoyance at once, but the prudent overlook an insult" (12:16). Wisdom is gained through seeking knowledge (see 18:15), taking advice, and accepting discipline (see 19:20).

The Certainty of Wisdom

While intelligence may be an illusion, wisdom is certain. Those who have it appreciate its value. When God invited King Solomon to ask for anything he would like, Solomon asked for wisdom (see 1 Kings 3:5–9). God was so pleased with this request that not only did he give him a "wise and discerning heart," but he also gave him what he had not asked for: wealth and honor, ensuring he would have "no equal among kings" in his lifetime (vv. 10–13).

We recognize wisdom by understanding what it looks like. It involves making the most of every day and understanding

God's will (see Ephesians 5:15–17). True, age brings wisdom, and with life experiences comes understanding (see Job 12:12). But young people can be biblically wise as well. Paul encouraged Timothy, "Don't let anyone look down on you because you are young, but set an example for the believers in speech, in conduct, in love, in faith and in purity" (1 Timothy 4:12).

Wisdom is visible through appearance: "A person's wisdom brightens their face and changes its hard appearance" (Ecclesiastes 8:1), and it's reflected in behavior: "Who is wise and understanding among you? Let them show it by their good life, by deeds done in the humility that comes from wisdom" (James 3:13). James describes wisdom from heaven as "first of all pure; then peace-loving, considerate, submissive, full of mercy and good fruit, impartial and sincere" (v. 17). Wise people are cool-headed and composed. "Fools give full vent to their rage, but the wise bring calm in the end" (Proverbs 29:11).

We also reveal wisdom through our words. "The mouths of the righteous utter wisdom, and their tongues speak what is just" (Psalm 37:30). Jesus promised to give his disciples "words and wisdom that none of your adversaries will be able to resist or contradict" (Luke 21:15). But remember in judging character through conversation, wisdom is often revealed not through rambling but restraint: "The one who has knowledge uses words with restraint, and whoever has understanding is even-tempered. Even fools are thought wise if they keep silent, and discerning if they hold their tongues" (Proverbs 17:27–28). Word to the wise.

CHAPTER 21

THE FANTASY OF FIRST IMPRESSIONS

For we live by faith,
not by sight.
2 CORINTHIANS 5:7

Maria meets Max at a professional networking mixer. Tall, dark, and handsome, he is also eloquent and educated—judging from the string of degrees after his name. Assuming professional packaging predicts personality, Maria accepts both his business card and his invitation to a business lunch the next day.

Arriving first, Maria realizes that the elegant-sounding "Le Chateau" is a corner deli, which Max explains has the "best steak sandwich in the city." He arrives late, apologizing that he had to take the bus because his sports car is in the shop. When their server forgets to charge them for their beverages, Max smiles and lays down barely enough cash to cover the tab, remarking that the drinks are apparently "on the house."

Three months later, Maria is missing a credit card, cash, and her grandmother's jewelry. It's too bad that she missed all of the red flags on her first date with Max, who has already cashed in on the items Maria has at least *noticed* are missing. We find much more before the first day of trial, when Max shows up in court wearing the same monogrammed suit that he wore the first evening Maria and he met. He is again dressed to make a great first impression but this time for the jury.

There is much more to judgment than what is visible or audible. "He will not judge by what he sees with his eyes, or decide by what he hears with his ears; but with righteousness he will judge the needy, with justice he will give decisions for the poor of the earth" (Isaiah 11:3–4). The key for us, with our limited knowledge, is to resist jumping to conclusions based on first impressions and gain as much information as we can by observing a person over time.

Lifestyle: Personality Revealed

If first impressions were always accurate, I would be out of a job. People are deceived by what they think they see and often what they want to see, allowing crafty criminals to cultivate an image that simulates charisma and chemistry. Some child predators look like Mr. Rogers but live like Peter Pan, letting your child enjoy privileges that you do not allow. From ice cream for breakfast to playing ball in the house to watching adult enter-tainment, the red flags are not evident through the way they look but how they live.

I have prosecuted people who were blue-suited, white-collar executives by day, traffickers by night, using sep-arate residences to live a double life. Sometimes the trappings of wealth conceal the underbelly of filth. We make assumptions about other people based on the clothes they wear, the cars they drive, and the zip codes in which they live. But fame and fortune cannot be feigned forever. A false façade is hard to maintain. The more you know, ask, or seek to discover over time, the more clearly a person's true identity is exposed.

> The more you know, ask, or seek to discover over time, the more clearly a person's true identity is exposed.

While anyone can dress the part, the environment sup-plies the rest of the story. You learn more about someone who gives you an unplanned lift by examining the state of their car than the quality of their clothes. Because for many of us, our vehicle is our home away from home and often filled with evi-dence of the way we live our lives. With suspects, a vehicle's interior can be a rolling crime scene containing everything from drugs to guns. With potential suitors, sunglasses or lipstick in the front seat might indicate an existing relationship, while a car seat in the back reveals a young family. Demeanor deceives, but patterns predict the person. We can't just examine behavior on a single occasion but consistently over time.

The Test of Time

As a career sex crimes prosecutor, I am used to arguing that "patterns make the predator." But the premise is the same in any situation: behavior reveals true colors over time. Sometimes, investigators do not discover the individuals involved in a crime scene through a photograph but through forensics. I have handled cases where the jury's verdict hinged on the mixture of DNA profiles present in a single drop of blood—representing who was in a certain location during a snapshot in time. But just as jurors also need to know why the individuals were present, we need more than a snapshot in time to explore the personality behind the presence.

Sometimes charges do not capture the character behind the criminal activity. I have prosecuted petite women accused of committing low-level misdemeanors who were so hostile and threatening outside the courtroom that an armed investigator had to accompany me to court. On the other hand, I have prosecuted sizable, imposing men charged with murder, mayhem, and torture who behaved like perfect gentlemen. Some people wear their intentions on their sleeves; others mask malevolence with mild manners. But over time, true colors emerge.

Some people might fool us initially with a false front, but eventually, "Each tree is recognized by its own fruit" (Luke

6:44). Some people embody the fruit of the Spirit: "love, joy, peace, forbearance, kindness, goodness, faithfulness, gentleness and self-control" (Galatians 5:22–23). Fruit of the Spirit is contrasted with acts of the flesh, described by Paul in his letter to the Galatians as "obvious: sexual immorality, impurity and debauchery; idolatry and witchcraft; hatred, discord, jealousy, fits of rage, selfish ambition, dissensions, factions and envy; drunkenness, orgies, and the like" (vv. 19–21). Paul warns that people who "live like this will not inherit the kingdom of God" (v. 21).

Paul's choice of words is significant. He is intentionally distinguishing between suffering a lapse in judgment and intentionally making a choice in lifestyle. It's true that good people, on occasion, might lose their temper, selfishly desire success, or tie on one too many at the bar. Many new Christians are diamonds in the rough who need refining. But someone who adopts one or more of these acts of the flesh as a *way of living* will be recognized by their works and likely their words as well. Steer clear.

CHAPTER 22

THE PERILS OF POWER

What good is it for someone to gain the whole world,
yet forfeit their soul?
MARK 8:36

"Congratulations, you made it!" Employees who have spent years climbing the corporate ladder are heralded by their peers once they attain a position of prominence. For some people, status and influence allow them to humbly lead from their heart. For others, power goes straight to their head.

From disgraced CEOs to dethroned world leaders, history is riddled with examples in which power has led to corruption. Intoxicated with influence, some succumb to a euphoric but false sense of invincibility: "In his pride the wicked man does not seek him; in all his thoughts there is no room for God" (Psalm 10:4).

In teaching sexual harassment prevention, I include research describing the link between a sudden rise to power and

145

sexually aggressive behavior in both men and women.[22] Men with a low amount of power who are suddenly placed in a position of high power may display increased hostility when rejected by an attractive woman, and both men and women with chronically low power rising to high power are more likely to admit an inclination to "inappropriately pursue an unrequited workplace attraction."[23]

High power can be abused by exploiting power dynamics as well. The #MeToo movement exposed how perpetrators use power as both sword and shield, facilitating despicable behavior and providing protection from accountability. What is it about power that can cause this behavior? Sometimes, it's the danger of pride.

Power and Pride

"It's good to be the king" is a tongue-in-cheek catchphrase popularized by advertisers, singers, and a 1981 Mel Brooks comedy touting the benefits of being the boss. But not all kings would agree; their success often depends on how they experience and understand the power they have. Babylonian King Nebuchadnezzar was driven away from his kingdom and forced to live with the wild animals, eating grass and drenched with dew, until he acknowledged the sovereignty of God (see Daniel 4:28–34). King Herod was struck down by an angel after he failed to give praise to God after giving a public speech (see Acts 12:21–23).

Pride of the heart can be deceitful for those feeling powerful and living "on the heights" who ask themselves, "Who can bring me down to the ground?" (Obadiah 1:3). Indeed, King Nebuchadnezzar's humbling stemmed from his own self-aggrandizing thoughts while he was walking on the roof of his royal palace (see Daniel 4:29–30).

But pride is not always wrong. There are times when we are right to take pride in ourselves, if we first test our own actions without concern for how we measure up to others (see Galatians 6:4). And we may take pride in the accomplishment of others, as Paul's great pride in the Corinthians left him joyful and greatly encouraged (see 2 Corinthians 7:4).

Power is not earned but received. When Pontius Pilate told Jesus he had the authority to release or crucify him, Jesus reminded him, "You would have no power over me if it were not given to you from above" (John 19:11). Paul reminds the Corinthians of the same truth through his questions: "For who makes you different from anyone else? What do you have that you did not receive? And if you did receive it, why do you boast as though you did not?" (1 Corinthians 4:7).

Ultimately, we are to impress not each other but God. "Am I now trying to win the approval of human beings, or of God? Or am I trying to please people? If I were still trying to please people, I would not be a servant of Christ" (Galatians 1:10).

The Benevolent Use of Power

Power does not always corrupt; sometimes it creates the opportunity to empower others. This is important because, without good leadership, people are left to moral wanderings, as during the period when "Israel had no king" and "everyone did as they saw fit" (Judges 21:25).

Instead of dictating, benevolent leaders encourage their followers by wielding positive influence, which inspires affirmative change. They don't exploit power; they pay it forward.

God gave us a spirit not of fear but of power, love, and self-control (see 2 Timothy 1:7). Paul rejoices, "I can do all this through him who gives me strength" (Philippians 4:13), encouraging us to "be strong in the Lord and in his mighty power" (Ephesians 6:10). Wisdom is power; it "makes one wise person more powerful than ten rulers in a city" (Ecclesiastes 7:19).

Godly power is a gift. The Lord "gives strength to the weary and increases the power of the weak" (Isaiah 40:29). Isaiah further reminds us that "even youths grow tired and weary, and young men stumble and fall; but those who hope in the LORD will renew their strength." (vv. 30–31).

True power is perfected in weakness. When Paul complained about an ongoing infirmity, the Lord reminded him, "My grace is sufficient for you, for my power is made perfect in weakness" (2 Corinthians 12:9). Paul went on to proclaim that he delighted "in weaknesses, in insults, in hardships, in persecutions, in difficulties," recognizing that "when I am weak, then I am strong" (v. 10).

True power is perfected in weakness.

Jesus gave his disciples "authority to trample on snakes and scorpions and to overcome all the power of the enemy" (Luke 10:19) and promised his followers, "you will receive power when the Holy Spirit comes on you; and you will be my witnesses in Jerusalem, and in all Judea and Samaria, and to the ends of the earth" (Acts 1:8). As the one true source of power, Jesus "is able to do immeasurably more than all we ask or imagine, according to his power that is at work within us" (Ephesians 3:20).

CHAPTER 23

THE RAPTURE OF RICHES

Be on your guard against all kinds of greed;
life does not consist in an abundance of possessions.

LUKE 12:15

Who Wants to Marry a Multi-Millionaire? was a reality show in which fifty women competed for the "privilege" of marrying a wealthy man they had never seen—except in silhouette. The marriage between the man and the winning contestant, performed at the end of the show, was annulled after the honeymoon. Although most people don't select partners based solely on money, the flagrant glorification of wealth was no doubt a powerful influence on the 22 million people who watched the broadcast. And not in a positive way.

When it comes to popularity, money matters. "The poor are shunned even by their neighbors, but the rich have many friends" (Proverbs 14:20). But while "wealth attracts many

150

friends" (19:4), it does not always attract the right kind of people. Wealthy people are relentlessly hounded for donations from family, friends, and even foes. Some of the richest people downplay their worth to avoid being targeted by those who seek to exploit and manipulate for money.

People of modest means might not appreciate the extent to which wealth creates unique stressors, not the least of which is concern about losing what you have. "Cast but a glance at riches, and they are gone, for they will surely sprout wings and fly off to the sky like an eagle" (23:5).

And borrowing the analogy of the professional "rat race," chasing wealth is exhausting. Proverbs 23 further advises us, "Do not wear yourself out to get rich; do not trust your own cleverness" (v. 4). Many people with high-paying jobs complain they have no time to enjoy the money they earn because they are too busy working to make more. And they have no plans to slow down, joking that they are destined to die at their desks. I know some who have, and it's a shame.

The Dark Side of Wealth

We know the best things in life are free. But we also appreciate that while money can't buy us love, it can pay our bills, keep our furnace running, and keep the lights on. Money is not the problem; it is our attitude toward affluence that is dangerous. "Whoever loves money never has enough; whoever loves wealth is never satisfied with their income" (Ecclesiastes 5:10). And whoever loves wealth cannot also serve God: "You cannot serve both God and money" (Matthew 6:24; Luke 16:13). As many people have learned the hard way, love of money creates heartache. "Some people, eager for money, have wandered from the faith and pierced themselves with many griefs" (1 Timothy 6:10).

One consequence of having riches is the temptation to show them off. After God miraculously healed King Hezekiah of an illness when he was on the brink of death, the king faced judgment for the manner in which he received Babylonian envoys—who ironically had come to see him because they heard he was sick. Instead of sharing his miraculous healing, Hezekiah showed off his riches: "The silver, the gold, the spices and the fine olive oil—his armory and everything found among his treasures. There was nothing in his palace or in all his kingdom that Hezekiah did not show them" (2 Kings 20:13).

As a result, the prophet Isaiah informed him, "The time will surely come when everything in your palace, and all that your predecessors have stored up until this day, will be carried off to Babylon. Nothing will be left" (v. 17). The desire for wealth is not only pointless, but it is also dangerous spiritually, emotionally, and, ironically, even financially.

From Riches to Ruin

Many lottery winners go broke. Reasons include financial mismanagement, foolish spending, and hefty taxes. Many winners lose more than the money as family and friends inundate them with hostile demands, expecting a share of the pie and writing them off if they refuse to write a check. Some lotto winners even have trouble making new friends because when they upgrade their zip code, their new neighbors look down on them for not having earned their wealth.

And because most lottery winners are not permitted to remain anonymous, they also live in fear of being targeted by thieves and scammers. Taken together, the stress and pressure of managing sudden, unexpected wealth take a toll both mentally and morally, leading some winners to shift priorities in the wrong direction. Some admit that had they known what type of person they would become and everything they would lose after they won, they would have torn up the ticket.

Money and Morality

Gaining wealth is often linked with losing morality. "They have become rich and powerful and have grown fat and sleek. Their evil deeds have no limit; they do not seek justice" (Jeremiah 5:27–28). King Solomon recognized this in his wisdom: "Give me neither poverty nor riches, but give me only my daily bread. Otherwise, I may have too much and disown you and say, 'Who is the Lord?'" (Proverbs 30:8–9). For many people, wealth threatens faith. It is not that people have not heard the Word of God, but as explained in the parable of the sower, when sown among thorns, "the worries of this life and the deceitfulness of wealth choke the word, making it unfruitful" (Matthew 13:22).

In addition, money can create pride. "By your wisdom and understanding you have gained wealth for yourself and amassed gold and silver in your treasuries. By your great skill in trading you have increased your wealth, and because of your wealth your heart has grown proud" (Ezekiel 28:4–5). We forget where wealth actually comes from: "Remember the LORD your God, for it is he who gives you the ability to produce wealth" (Deuteronomy 8:18).

Wealth is also linked with exploitive relationships, pursued by "gold diggers" and others seeking to manipulate for personal gain. "The rich rule over the poor, and the borrower is slave to the lender" (Proverbs 22:7). James 5:1–6 provides a warning to rich oppressors who lived in "luxury and self-indulgence," hoarding wealth. They are warned that, because they failed to pay their employees and condemned the innocent, misery is coming: "Your wealth has rotted, and moths have eaten your clothes. Your gold and silver are corroded. Their corrosion will testify against you and eat your flesh like fire."

Show Me Your Wallet

Purse strings reflect priorities. Like the widow's offering in Mark 12:41–44, it is what people do with their money that reveals their heart. Watching crowds donate to the temple treasury, Jesus noted that while many rich people contributed out of their abundance, a poor widow offered more than all the others because she gave everything she had to live on (see vv. 43–44).

But rich people can be generous too. Some wealthy employers share their wealth with loyal, industrious employees, whom they invite to "come and share your master's happiness!" (Matthew 25:23). Although we cannot judge integrity through income, we can discern what people consider to be important because our treasure and our heart tend to be in the same place (see Luke 12:34; Matthew 6:21).

Purse strings reflect priorities.

In speaking with a rich young man seeking eternal life, Jesus explained the difference between worldly wealth and heavenly wealth: "If you want to be perfect, go, sell your possessions and give to the poor, and you will have treasure in heaven. Then come, follow me" (Matthew 19:21). When the man turned and walked away sad, Jesus shared the famous revelation: "It is easier for a camel to go through the eye of a needle than for someone who is rich to enter the kingdom of God" (v. 24). Instead, the words of Scripture advise us to keep our lives free from the love of money and to be content with what we have: God's presence and protection (see Hebrews 13:5).

True Prosperity Is Priceless

King Solomon had everything a king could want: riches, power, wives, children, livestock. But he also had wisdom. Accordingly, he described his life of abundance as "utterly meaningless!" (Ecclesiastes 1:2). Why? Think about a time in your own life when you were truly happy and consider what brought you such joy. Perhaps it was the birth of a child or the day your spouse proposed. Or perhaps it was just time spent with family at the beach or a park. What was the price tag on those experiences? For most of us, the answer is *zero*. You could own one of the most impressive multi-million-dollar homes or yachts in the world, but if you had to live there alone, cut off from communication with your loved ones, you would be miserable.

And the Bible consistently reminds us of the uncertainty of wealth: "The rich should take pride in their humiliation—since they will pass away like a wild flower" (James 1:10). Accordingly, Paul cautions us not to set our hopes on the uncertainty of riches but on God, "who richly provides us with everything for our enjoyment." If we are rich in good deeds, generous and ready to share, we are storing up treasure for a firm foundation for the future (1 Timothy 6:17–19).

Many things are more important than money. "A good name is more desirable than great riches; to be esteemed is better than silver or gold" (Proverbs 22:1). "Wisdom is more precious than rubies, and nothing you desire can compare with her" (8:11). Comparing the protection of wisdom to that of wealth, the advantage of wisdom is that it "preserves those who have it" (Ecclesiastes 7:12). If you are blessed with wealth, the most effective path to personal prosperity is to use it to bless others.

CHAPTER 24

THE LURE OF LUXURY

*Give her as much torment and grief
as the glory and luxury she gave herself.*
REVELATION 18:7

The TV show *Lifestyles of the Rich and Famous* became famous in the mid-1980s. It portrayed extravagant lifestyles, luxurious living, and all of the trappings of wealth. It did not cover depression, drugs, suicide, gambling, addiction, betrayal, or many of the other hazards of "having it all." People who actually own multi-million-dollar homes or yachts are constantly bombarded with requests to host parties, events, and fundraisers without regard for their desire to enjoy private time with their families like "normal" people do. And extravagance does not guarantee happiness.

Splendor is not necessarily sustainable. Jesus demonstrated this by his words as he was leaving the temple. When one of his disciples declared, "Look, Teacher! What massive stones! What magnificent buildings!" Jesus replied, "Do you see all these great buildings?" followed by the pronouncement of impending destruction: "Not one stone here will be left on another; every one will be thrown down" (Mark 13:1–2). Grandeur and greatness can be tempting but temporary.

In the cases I prosecute, luxury is often a lure. Human traffickers entice innocent young women into what they believe will be a glamorous subculture involving expensive clothes, designer bags, hotel rooms, limo rides…and selling their bodies for sex. Impressionable youths from depressed areas who lack access to living essentials are particularly vulnerable to this type of exploitation. The chance to have nice things and experience the trappings of wealth for the first time can be an opportunity too good to pass up, which tragically devolves into a life of vice.

The Optics of Opulence

"Not in my backyard" is a popular myth I seek to debunk in the human trafficking prevention programs I frequently conduct, referring to the belief that such activity does not occur in upscale communities. White picket fences around expensive homes on tree-lined streets do not preclude the presence of perversion. On the contrary, expensive neighborhoods often provide the perfect cover for criminal activity. Because decadence disguises depravity.

Misjudging the neighborhood was an issue in Old Testament times as well. When Abram asked his nephew Lot to choose which portion of the land he wanted to have for himself, Lot "looked around" and chose an area that was "well watered, like the garden of the LORD," not knowing he had chosen an area that contained Sodom, where people were described as "wicked" (Genesis 13:9–13). In fact, Sodom and neighboring city Gomorrah were so evil that God destroyed them along with all living things in and around them by raining down burning sulfur (see 19:24–25).

How could an area that looked so pleasing be so poisonous? Anyone who has ever lived in a gorgeous neighborhood only to learn of a drug house down the block can attest to the charade of curb appeal. Appearances can be deceiving whether we're judging options that are romantic or residential.

When Depravity Looks Dashing

A sleek white sedan pulls up to a five-star restaurant valet station, and two well-dressed men alight sporting Armani suits. They are so accustomed to being treated like royalty that they don't hesitate to turn the car over to the valet while they treat themselves to a steak dinner…even though there is a body in the trunk, a man they stabbed to death earlier in the day. The luxury car with the corpse is waiting for them right out front when they finish, the valet having selected the spot to showcase the caliber of the restaurant clientele.

The perception of prosperity creates a positive perception, but a gilded exterior can conceal inner greed and guilt. Some high-powered executives and businesspeople live a life of apparent luxury that hides the wickedness of their ways. But not if you know what to look for. Manner of living does not guarantee proper manners; it is the way a person spends their time that reveals the condition of their heart.

> Manner of living does not guarantee proper manners;
> it is the way a person spends their time that reveals
> the condition of their heart.

Again, Jeffrey Epstein is a prime example. He hosted politicians and celebrities from around the globe who were enamored with his lavish lifestyle. Planes, islands, mansions, he had it all. But his elite image insulated him from closer scrutiny, causing people to be smitten instead of suspicious. Behind the scenes, sexual abuse was occurring within the decorated halls of wealth.

Even after his conviction in 2008, when he was required to register as a sex offender, Mr. Epstein retained his A-list status, as did his associate, British socialite Ghislaine Maxwell. She was later convicted in 2021 as Epstein's partner in crime after a jury trial exposed the deviance behind the affluence.

When Less Is More

Extravagance itself is not evil. Biblical kings both good and bad lived lives of luxury, with some of the most lavish descriptions befitting righteous royalty, such as King David and his son King Solomon. But in many cases, less is more. Jesus Christ never slept in a king-size bed, irony intended. As he explained himself, "Foxes have dens and birds have nests, but the Son of Man has no place to lay his head" (Luke 9:58). John the Baptist lived in the wilderness, clothed in camel's hair and a leather belt (see Matthew 3:4). After noting John was not a "man dressed in fine clothes," as "those who wear fine clothes are in kings' palaces," Jesus described John as a great prophet (11:8–11).

Worldly prosperity does not guarantee security or longevity. The parable of the rich fool illustrates the deceitfulness and worthlessness of abundant living. After having built bigger barns to store surplus grain, a farmer tells himself, "You have plenty of grain laid up for many years. Take life easy; eat, drink and be merry," only to have his life demanded from him that very night, leaving all of his possessions to others (Luke 12:16–20). "This is how it will be with whoever stores up things for themselves but is not rich toward God" (v. 21). Better to share the wealth.

CHAPTER 25

WHEN BUSYNESS
LOOKS LIKE BUSINESS

*Be very careful, then, how you live—not as unwise but as wise,
making the most of every opportunity, because the days are evil.*
EPHESIANS 5:15–16

Everyone understands the value of hard work. Indeed, the proverbial wife of noble character "watches over the affairs of her household and does not eat the bread of idleness" (Proverbs 31:27). "Laziness brings on deep sleep, and the shiftless go hungry" (19:15). But as anyone knows who has had a job "pushing paper," there is a difference between activity and productivity.

Staying active fills a void for many people—whether they are accomplishing anything or not. Some people fill their time with distraction to escape unpleasant thoughts or feelings. There is nothing wrong with staying busy. But the question needs to be:

Busy doing what? Tedious, monotonous, worthless tasks are of no benefit in the long run and deplete time that we could better spend on achieving goals and enjoying life.

Jesus had a busy ministry, often working day and night. But he also took time to rest. When he and his disciples were overwhelmed by the number of people coming to see them to the point that they did not even have a break to eat, Jesus told them, "Come with me by yourselves to a quiet place and get some rest" (Mark 6:31). Resting benefits body, mind, and soul. Because our bodies are temples of God (see 1 Corinthians 6:19), we want to keep them healthy. But rest also benefits our mind. A rested brain also stimulates creativity, introspection, and memory.

One of the classic biblical passages about the perils of busyness is found in Luke 10, comparing the behavior of sisters Martha and Mary when Jesus came to visit. Martha was busy, "distracted by all the preparations that had to be made," while Mary sat at the feet of Jesus, listening to him speak. When Martha complained that Mary wasn't helping her, Jesus shed light on the situation, "Martha, Martha…you are worried and upset about many things, but few things are needed—or indeed only one. Mary has chosen what is better, and it will not be taken away from her" (vv. 38–42).

When Activity Is Unproductive

Multitasking is on its way to becoming the next Olympic sport. Yet when we try to perform many different tasks at once, we rarely succeed in performing any of them well. Divided attention creates distraction.

We learn the dangers of unproductive busyness in the first letter to Timothy, which warns that people "get into the habit of being idle and going about from house to house. And not only do they become idlers, but also busybodies who talk nonsense, saying things they ought not to" (5:13). Paul made the same type of distinction when he wrote to the Thessalonians, "We hear that some among you are idle and disruptive. They are not busy; they are busybodies" (2 Thessalonians 3:11).

Some people feel industrious when they fill their calendar with events and tasks but end up feeling totally overwhelmed. And chaos yields confusion, which is contrary to faith: "God is not a God of disorder but of peace" (1 Corinthians 14:33). Hectic lives produce headaches and heartache.

Productive activity requires the right mindset. Even wealthy people will not maintain an advantage simply because they are busy doing business. "For the sun rises with scorching heat and withers the plant; its blossom falls and its beauty is destroyed. In the same way, the rich will fade away even while they go about their business" (James 1:11). Perhaps we should consider a different perspective of value: "Show me, LORD, my life's end and the number of my days; let me know how fleeting my life is" (Psalm 39:4).

The Requirement of Rest

Regardless of our responsibilities, we are required to rest. The Ten Commandments reference resting in relation to keeping the Sabbath. "Remember the Sabbath day by keeping it holy. Six days you shall labor and do all your work, but the seventh day is a sabbath to the LORD your God. On it you shall not do any work, neither you, nor your son or daughter, nor your male or female servant, nor your animals, nor any foreigner residing in your towns" (Exodus 20:8–10). Jesus explained more fully, as Lord of the Sabbath (see Matthew 12:8), that "the Sabbath was made for man, not man for the Sabbath" (Mark 2:27).

Regardless of our responsibilities, we are required to rest.

Jesus invites anyone who is burdened or weary to come to him to find rest for our souls, because his "yoke is easy and [his] burden is light" (Matthew 11:28–30). Scripture advises us to cast all of our anxiety on him because he cares for each of us (see 1 Peter 5:7). Jesus also gives us the promise of peace: "You will keep in perfect peace those whose minds are steadfast, because they trust in you" (Isaiah 26:3). "Peace I leave with you; my peace I give you" (John 14:27).

The Lord describes the fruit of righteousness as peace, producing "quietness and confidence forever." He promises that his people will live in "peaceful dwelling places, in secure homes, in undisturbed places of rest" (Isaiah 32:17–18). Through prayer, petition, intercession, and thanksgiving, we endeavor to "live peaceful and quiet lives in all godliness and holiness" (1 Timothy 2:1–2). A healthy work-life balance does not balance busyness and bustle but productivity and peace.

CHAPTER 26

THE TEMPTATIONS OF TECHNOLOGY

Let us consider how we may spur one another on toward love and good deeds, not giving up meeting together, as some are in the habit of doing, but encouraging one another.

HEBREWS 10:24–25

Depending on your perspective, the COVID-19 pandemic restrictions felt like either a staycation or house arrest. For introverts, the silver lining was the opportunity to spend more time in their favorite place: home. Post-pandemic, having become tech-savvy in record time, those able to telework decided to maintain a home office, saving both time and gas by skipping the commute.

Some teleworkers joked that they could no longer fit into their work clothes anyway because they gained the dreaded

"Covid 19 (pounds)." In many cases, the extra poundage was due to both overeating and underactivity. Sitting in a chair for a day's worth of Zoom meetings followed by a virtual happy hour is not a healthy lifestyle, physically or emotionally.

But there is a greater compromise when we fail to gather in person. The Lord designed us to live in community and urged us not to give up meeting together (see Hebrews 10:25). Meeting "together" as small squares on the same Zoom screen doesn't count. There is value in remaining connected any way we can, but time, travel, and cost permitting, remote relationships should be the exception to the rule.

When Not Seeing Is Believing

Maria meets Thomas on a Christian dating site, where his impressive educational profile and handsome photos showcase an aspiring medical student with both charm and charisma. Assuming a Christian physician-in-training would be talented and trustworthy, she agrees to meet him for a first date. Unfortunately, she agrees to a "house call" dinner at her apartment instead of meeting in a public place. Sadly, the next house call she receives that night is from the police after she reports the rape.

Most of us in law enforcement have handled some version of this crime and warn others that misjudging someone based on the words of an online profile can be more than disappointing; it can be dangerous. Intelligent, often well-educated victims frequently realize the same thing in retrospect. They ask the same question: "Why didn't I see the red flags?" In many cases, they chose to begin a relationship because they believed what they read online. But virtual descriptions can be deceiving. Most people don't take the time to fact-check dating profiles; and even if they did, we can't fact-check personal preferences, such as professed religious beliefs. It is only when you get to know someone offline that you can tell if they practice what they preach.

We make the same mistakes when choosing friends. If I asked you to sit down and make a list of three hundred of your friends, could you do it? Probably not. But the average number of friends people have on Facebook is well over that amount. So who are these people? In reality, Facebook "friends" are acquaintances with whom we became connected over the years, often through contacts in common or because they had an attractive profile photo. If you wanted to update your cyber contact list, you would have to actually know your friends, as opposed to their avatar, in order to separate the authentic from the counterfeit, to accurately recognize character and compassion in companionship. A task that is much easier to do in person.

Keeping It Real

Virtual platforms were a part of life during the pandemic and allowed professionals to continue to work, students to learn, and family and friends to see each other. But we were not designed to toil and study in isolation, and superficial mingling with disembodied avatars should not constitute the extent of our social life.

Yet in a post-pandemic world, many people have become overly reliant on technology to the extent that, now that we are able to meet together again, some people don't want to. But spending too much time online surfing instead of offline socializing puts us out of touch. Healthy relationships are up close and personal, not virtual. Just ask our precious young people who spent most of the pandemic living behind a Zoom screen. And for adults, while teleworking saves time and gas money by skipping the commute, at what expense?

Healthy relationships are up close and personal, not virtual.

The Bible is filled with countless examples of the power of presence. God designed instruction to take place in person. "Assemble the people—men, women and children, and the foreigners residing in your towns—so they can listen and learn to fear the LORD your God and follow carefully all the words of this law" (Deuteronomy 31:12–13). Orderly worship is supposed to take place in person: "When you come together, each of you has a hymn, or a word of instruction, a revelation, a tongue or an interpretation" (1 Corinthians 14:26). When the Holy Spirit visited the believers at Pentecost, "they were all together in one place" (Acts 2:1).

Recognizing the value of sharing in person, churches were one of the institutions most resistant to moving totally online during the pandemic due to the lack of opportunities for meaningful, in-person fellowship. Inspiration and encouragement are essential for a healthy faith community. "Let us consider how we may spur one another on toward love and good deeds, not giving up meeting together" (Hebrews 10:24–25). Corporate worship is challenging online because singing and praising God is something we should experience in community. "Let the message of Christ dwell among you richly as you teach and admonish one another with all wisdom through psalms, hymns, and songs from the Spirit, singing to God with gratitude in your hearts" (Colossians 3:16).

Breaking Bread and Bonding

Making the best of a bad situation, we shared pandemic meals and beverages through a tiny camera on our computer screen during forced social restrictions. But we were not designed to eat and drink alone. Jesus did not share the Last Supper with his disciples online, nor did he feed the five thousand with five loaves of bread and two fish (see Matthew 14:13–21) by ordering through a food delivery app. Breaking bread is an activity we are to enjoy in person as an important element of the Christian life (see Acts 2:42, 46; 20:7). During his final meal with his disciples, while at the table, Jesus "took bread, gave thanks and broke it, and gave it to them, saying, 'This is my body given for you; do this in remembrance of me'" (Luke 22:19). The Last Supper was not a potluck.

Sharing meals together is one of the ways that faith involves fellowship. The New Testament is filled with examples of Jesus eating meals with others, from friends (see John 12:2) to foes (see Luke 14:1). He emphasized the value of inviting others to break bread together, especially those less privileged: "When you give a luncheon or dinner, do not invite your friends, your brothers or sisters, your relatives, or your rich neighbors; if you do, they may invite you back and so you will be repaid. But when you give a banquet, invite the poor, the crippled, the lame, the blind, and you will be blessed" (vv. 12–14).

Following the ministry of Jesus, as the early Christian community grew, they continued to meet together (see Acts 2:42–46). "All the believers were together and had everything in common" (v. 44). "Every day they continued to meet together in the temple courts. They broke bread in their homes and ate together with glad and sincere hearts" (v. 46). Let us emulate the joyful fellowship of the early Christians and enjoy life by celebrating friends, faith, and fellowship, offline.

CONCLUSION

The eye is the lamp of the body.
If your eyes are healthy,
your whole body will be full of light.
MATTHEW 6:22

Seeing is believing. The key is using the right lens to interpret what you see. As a career prosecutor and former defense attorney, having worked within the criminal justice system for over a quarter of a century, many people ask me if I have become cynical and jaded. The opposite is true. Pursuing justice involves consistent exposure to countless individuals who have dedicated their time and talent to making the world a better place.

Perfecting perspective requires the optics of optimism. Because mindset matters. Having discussed all of the reasons that bad can look good, we recognize that sometimes, depending on our state of mind and preconceptions, good can look bad. If our perspective is warped by negative experiences or stereotypes that lead us to assume the worst about people or situations, then we miss out on some of the most fulfilling experiences that life has to offer.

Developing a healthy mindset takes discipline. "Whatever is true, whatever is noble, whatever is right, whatever is pure, whatever is lovely, whatever is admirable—if anything is excellent or praiseworthy—think about such things" (Philippians 4:8). This is more than a "garbage in, garbage out" mentality. An intentional emphasis on meditating on positive thoughts goes far above and beyond a warning about what type of content to avoid. Celebrating positivity and viewing people and situations optimistically presents the world in a fresh light.

Celebrating positivity and viewing people and situations optimistically presents the world in a fresh light.

Practice Makes Perfect

As we've learned, the ability to distinguish bad from good requires practice and perception. In the same way trained investigators can spot counterfeit money because they know how to recognize the real thing, reading the Bible will enhance your ability to spot signs of inauthenticity. By improving your ability to both look and listen, you can better perceive the substance beneath the surface.

Spiritual maturity is described as becoming trained to distinguish good from evil (see Hebrews 5:14). This standard of excellence will help us see people and situations clearly. The good news is that, ultimately, we are not destined to suffer the downfall of deception. "Whoever walks in integrity walks securely, but whoever takes crooked paths will be found out" (Proverbs 10:9). Our goal, however, is to read the warning signs sooner rather than later, before our reading glasses become rose-colored, causing red flags to become pleasantly muted.

When it comes to evaluating a person or situation, you are most observant when you are objective. So whether you are considering a new profession or a new paramour, plan for perception. Before you act, consider and reflect on the following:

- **Why do you want this?** "When you ask, you do not receive, because you ask with wrong motives, that you may spend what you get on your pleasures" (James 4:3).

- **How does it make you feel?** "Take delight in the LORD, and he will give you the desires of your heart" (Psalm 37:4).

- **What makes this attractive?** "People look at the outward appearance, but the LORD looks at the heart" (1 Samuel 16:7).

- **When do you have to decide?** "Desire without knowledge is not good—how much more will hasty feet miss the way!" (Proverbs 19:2).

- **Who is encouraging you to do this?** "Although they know God's righteous decree that those who do such things deserve death, they not only continue to do these very things but also approve of those who practice them" (Romans 1:32).

- **Who would disapprove and why?** "Whoever rebukes a person will in the end gain favor rather than one who has a flattering tongue" (Proverbs 28:23).

- **How will this improve your life?** "Whether you eat or drink or whatever you do, do it all for the glory of God" (1 Corinthians 10:31).

- **How will you use it to improve the lives of others?** "Do nothing out of selfish ambition or vain conceit. Rather, in humility value others above yourselves" (Philippians 2:3).

- **How will this impact your image or reputation?** "Let your light shine before others, that they may see your good deeds and glorify your Father in heaven" (Matthew 5:16).

Learning to distinguish healthy from harmful desires allows you to distinguish the lure of the world from the truth of the Word. While others are seeking fame or fortune, love or luxury, be wise enough to "seek first his kingdom and his righteousness, and all these things will be given to you as well" (6:33).

When Bad Becomes Good

In the Old Testament, the Lord gave a message to the prophet Ezekiel about his plans for the people of Israel: "I will give them an undivided heart and put a new spirit in them; I will remove from them their heart of stone and give them a heart of flesh" (Ezekiel 11:19). When people change, so do their desires. "Let the wicked forsake their ways and the unrighteous their thoughts" (Isaiah 55:7). "Anyone who has been stealing must steal no longer, but must work, doing something useful with their own hands, that they may have something to share with those in need" (Ephesians 4:28). A changed life creates a changed lifestyle.

Paul reminds the Colossians that because they have been raised with Christ, they no longer walk in the old ways, in the lives they once lived (see Colossians 3:1–7). That they have rid themselves of "anger, rage, malice, slander, and filthy language" because they have shed their old selves and "put on the new self, which is being renewed in knowledge in the image of its Creator" (vv. 8–10).

A Checkered Past to a Bright Future

Before a criminal defendant is sentenced, both sides have the opportunity to address circumstances in aggravation and mitigation. One consistent factor for consideration is the defendant's potential for rehabilitation: the potential for a bright future despite a dark past. With Jesus, this is possible for everyone.

The Bible is full of colorful characters who, despite a history of greed or ill-repute, confessed and repented. There is nothing about a dubious past that prevents a positive future. While teaching in the temple courts, Jesus informed the chief priests and the elders of the people that "the tax collectors and the prostitutes are entering the kingdom of God ahead of you" because they believed the words of John the Baptist (Matthew 21:31). Many people with regrettable histories are enormously receptive to the promise of forgiveness and a new lease on life— sometimes specifically because they have the most to gain.

Luke 7:36–50 describes how a woman who had "lived a sinful life" approached Jesus when he was eating at a Pharisee's house, bringing an alabaster jar of perfume. While weeping, she washed his feet with her tears and dried them with her hair, kissing them and pouring perfume on them. When the Pharisee hosting Jesus, whose name was Simon, thought that if Jesus were a prophet, then he would know the woman was a sinner, Jesus compared her behavior to that of his host:

> "I came into your house. You did not give me any water for my feet, but she wet my feet with her tears and wiped them with her hair. You did not give me a kiss, but this woman, from the time I entered, has not stopped kissing my feet. You did not put oil on my head, but she has poured perfume on my feet. Therefore, I tell you, her many sins have been forgiven—as her great love has shown. But whoever has been forgiven little loves little." (vv. 44–47)

Luke 19 introduces Zacchaeus, a rich chief tax collector. When Jesus announced he must stay at his house that day, Zacchaeus received him joyfully (vv. 5–6). Although the crowd grumbled that Jesus was going to be "the guest of a sinner," Zacchaeus announced a change of heart: "Here and now I give half of my possessions to the poor, and if I have cheated anybody out of anything, I will pay back four times the amount," to which Jesus declared, "Today salvation has come to this house" (vv. 7–9).

An Eternal Perspective

Biblical wisdom encourages us to view our circumstances in context: "There is a time for everything, and a season for every activity under the heavens" (Ecclesiastes 3:1). Regardless of our current situation, Paul assures us that "in all things God works for the good of those who love him, who have been called according to his purpose" (Romans 8:28). Contemporary times can be challenging and disappointing, as conflict and political pressures threaten the stability of peace and prosperity. But Scripture advises us not to conform to the pattern of the world but to be transformed by the renewing of our minds (see 12:2).

If you have been disappointed in relationships, people, or situations, consider a fresh perspective. Always stay vigilant for red flags but don't miss the green lights. Many people are genuinely as good as they look. Attractive and approachable, they are also kind, generous, trustworthy, and authentic. And healthy situations, opportunities, and adventures abound. My prayer is that each of you finds love and happiness in all areas of life through patience, perception, and biblical wisdom.

The L ORD bless you and keep you;
the L ORD make his face shine on you and be gracious to you;
the L ORD turn his face toward you and give you peace.

NUMBERS 6:24–26

ACKNOWLEDGMENTS

I would like to thank a special group of people for their inspiration and encouragement. Tom Phillips, who selflessly shared his advice and contacts to make this book possible. To the talented literary professionals at BroadStreet Publishing. And to my mother, Elizabeth Patrick, and sister, Jennifer Patrick, for their love and encouragement in this venture and all others.

ENDNOTES

1   Ellen Cranley and Benjamin Goggin, "The Life of Jeffrey Epstein, the Convicted Sex Offender and Well-Connected Financier Who Died in Jail Awaiting Sex Trafficking Charges," *Insider*, August 10, 2019, https://www.businessinsider.com/jeffrey-epstein-life-biography-net-worth-2019-7.

2   Ray Sanchez and Natisha Lance, "Judge Finds Michelle Carter Guilty of Manslaughter in Texting Suicide Case," CNN, updated June 17, 2017, https://www.cnn.com/2017/06/16/us/michelle-carter-texting-case/index.html.

3   Cranley and Goggin, "The Life of Jeffrey Epstein, the Convicted Sex Offender."

4   Christopher Klein, "Mobster Al Capone Ran a Soup Kitchen During the Great Depression," History.com, updated April 26, 2021, https://www.history.com/news/al-capone-great-depression-soup-kitchen.

5   Brad Smithfield, "Serial Killer Ted Bundy Once Worked at a Suicide Hotline Crisis Center," *The Vintage News*, November 1, 2016, https://www.thevintagenews.com/2016/11/01/serial-killer-ted-bundy-worked-suicide-hotline-crisis-center/.

6   Ginger E. Faulkner, Russell L. Kolts, and Gail F. Hicks, "Sex Role Ideology, Relationship Context, and Response to Sexual Coercion in College Females," *Sex Roles* 59, no. 3–4 (2008): 139–50. https://doi.org/10.1007/s11199-008-9435-1.

7   Faulkner, Kolts, and Hicks, "Sex Role Ideology, Relationship Context, and Response to Sexual Coercion in College Females."

8   William G. Graziano and Jennifer Weisho Bruce, "Attraction and the Initiation of Relationships: A Review of the Empirical Literature," in *Handbook of Relationship Initiation*, eds. Susan Sprecher, Amy Wenzel, and John Harvey (New York: Psychology Press, 2008), 269–95 (281).

9 *Encyclopedia Britannica*, s.v. "idolatry," accessed on July 19, 2022, https://www.britannica.com/topic/idolatry.

10 David M. Bierie and Paul J. Detar, "Geographic and Social Movement of Sex Offender Fugitives," *Crime & Delinquency* 62, no. 8 (2016): 983–1002, https://doi.org/10.1177/0011128714530658.

11 "X-rays of Evel Knievel's Broken Bones," Two Views, accessed on July 19, 2022, https://two-views.com/celebrity/evel-knievel-xrays.html.

12 Manya Steinkoler, "Lone Wolf Terrorists: Howling in the Eye of the Wind—The Case of Adam Lanza," *International Forum of Psychoanalysis* 26, no. 4 (January 2018): 217–25, https://doi.org/10.1080/0803706X.2017.1333142.

13 Joey Garrison and Alan Gomez, "Who Is Sol Pais? What We Know about the Woman Besotted by Columbine Shooting," *Coloradoan*, April 17, 2019, https://www.coloradoan.com/story/news/2019/04/17/sol-pais-columbine-shooting-colorado-threaten-schools/3497763002/.

14   Patricia Mazzei, "Who Was Sol Pais, the Woman Sought in Colorado?," *The New York Times* (website), April 17, 2019, https://www.nytimes.com/2019/04/17/us/sol-pais-columbine.html.

15   Meagan J. Brem et al., "Problematic Pornography Use and Physical and Sexual Intimate Partner Violence Perpetration among Men in Batterer Intervention Programs," *Journal of Interpersonal Violence* 36, no. 11–12 (June 2021): NP6085–6105, https://doi.org/10.1177/0886260518812806.

16   John D. Foubert and Ana J. Bridges, "What Is the Attraction? Pornography Use Motives in Relation to Bystander Intervention," *Journal of Interpersonal Violence* 32, no. 20 (October 2017): 3071–89, https://doi.org/10.1177/0886260515596538.

17   "New Women's Health Study Findings Recently Were Reported by Researchers at Virginia Commonwealth University (Pornography and Heterosexual Women's Intimate Experiences With a Partner)," *Women's Health Weekly*, June 13, 2019, 561. Gale OneFile: Military and Intelligence. https://link.gale.com/apps/doc/A588261361/PPMI?u=san96005&sid=bookmark-PPMI&xid=1a14002e.

18 Mariana A. Saramago, Jorge Cardoso, and Isabel Leal, "Pornography Use by Sex Offenders at the Time of the Index Offense: Characterization and Predictors," *Journal of Sex & Marital Therapy* 45, no. 6 (March 2019): 473–87, https://doi.org/10.1080/0092623X.2018.1562501.

19 Mark H. Butler et al., "Pornography Use and Loneliness: A Bidirectional Recursive Model and Pilot Investigation," *Journal of Sex & Marital Therapy* 44, no. 2 (February 2018): 127–37, https://doi.org/10.1080/0092623X.2017.1321601.

20 Alston Chase, "Harvard and the Making of the Unabomber," *The Atlantic* (website), June 2000, https://www.theatlantic.com/magazine/archive/2000/06/harvard-and-the-making-of-the-unabomber/378239/.

21 "James Holmes Was among Elite in Neuroscience before Aurora Theater Massacre," *The Denver Post* (website), updated May 1, 2016, https://www.denverpost.com/2012/08/04/james-holmes-was-among-elite-in-neuroscience-before-aurora-theater-massacre/.

22 Melissa J. Williams, Deborah H. Gruenfeld, and Lucia E. Guillory, "Sexual Aggression When Power Is New: Effects of Acute High Power on Chronically Low-Power Individuals," *Journal of Personality and Social Psychology* 112, no. 2 (2017): 201–23, https://doi:10.1037/pspi0000068.

23 Williams, Gruenfeld, and Guillory, "Sexual Aggression When Power Is New."

ABOUT THE AUTHOR

Dr. Wendy L. Patrick is career prosecutor who has completed more than 165 trials ranging from hate crimes to domestic violence to first-degree murder. Named the "Ronald M. George Public Lawyer of the Year" by the California State Bar's Public Law Section, she has been recognized by her peers as one of the top ten criminal attorneys in San Diego by the *San Diego Daily Transcript.* She is a certified instructor for law enforcement with the Institute of Criminal Investigation and a certified chaplain with the California Practical Chaplain Association.

Passionate about apologetics, Dr. Patrick uses her evidence-based persuasion skills to defend the faith. She holds a master of divinity degree from Bethel Seminary San Diego, where she received the "Excellence in Preaching" and "Zondervan Biblical Languages" awards. She earned her doctorate in theology from the University of Wales Trinity Saint David and is formally ordained as a Christian minister through Converge Worldwide. She also holds a biblical counseling certificate from Horizon College.

Dr. Patrick spoke on the subject of human trafficking at Faith and Law Around the Globe conferences in Hong Kong and South Africa and taught a course on human trafficking at Handong International Law School in South Korea. She regularly teaches sexual assault prevention for the United States Army, presenting programs domestically as well as in Bavaria and Germany.

Dr. Patrick is the former president of the Christian Legal Society Metro New York chapter, an elected member of the American Law Institute, and a member of the San Diego District Attorney Inter-Faith Advisory Board. She also sits on the Board of Directors for Pacific Theological Seminary.

Dr. Patrick appears on air daily with major news outlets including CNN, Fox News Channel, HLN, and FOX Business Network. She has her own radio show on KCBQ called *Today With Dr. Wendy*, a biweekly radio tour on Fox News Radio called *Weekly Legal*, and a weekly slot on both Fox 5 San Diego called *Inside the Law* and Real America's Voice News' *The Docket*. She had her own segment for years as a behavioral analyst on *Spotted*, Australia's Seven Network Morning Show, and she is a regular guest on *Crime Stories with Nancy Grace*. Dr. Patrick has guest anchored national television news on One America News, America Trends, and Newsmax and served as a regular guest host for KOGO radio San Diego for years.

Dr. Patrick has regular columns in *Psychology Today* and *Law Enforcement Quarterly*. She was a *Huffington Post* contributor and published her own ethics column in the *San Diego Daily Transcript* for more than a decade. She has been quoted in a variety of sources, such as *The New York Times, USA Today, US News and World Report, The Washington Post, Associated Press, Bloomberg Businessweek, CSNBC, CNN.com, FoxNews.com*, and *The Christian Science Monitor.* She has authored multiple articles in *The Christian Lawyer*, a publication of the Christian Legal Society.

Currently, Dr. Patrick is a professor of theology, law, and culture at Veritas International University, where she teaches Christian ethics, gospel and culture, interpersonal communications, and apologetics and the art of persuasion. She is also a course designer and instructor for Trinity Law School. She is a longtime faculty member at San Diego State University and regularly guest lectures at other educational institutions and Christian conferences.

On a personal note, Dr. Patrick holds a purple belt in Shorin-Ryu karate, is a concert violinist with the La Jolla Symphony, and plays the electric violin professionally with a rock band performing both locally and in Hollywood.